7 Tips for Coping Emotionally in an Uncertain World

Dr. Dacia P. Hastings Proctor

TheTalkDr

ISBN 979-8-88751-595-3 (paperback)
ISBN 979-8-88751-596-0 (digital)

Christian Faith Publishing
832 Park Avenue
Meadville, PA 16335
www.christianfaithpublishing.com

Printed in the United States of America

To my father, Charlesworth K. Hastings, who passed away at the time I was writing this book. He represented such quiet strength that I know he would have wanted me to finish this book even during my period of grief.

To my mother, who has incredible faith in God and always taught us how to pray and trust in God.

To my husband, Antwan, my best friend, my person, and my place of comfort, for always giving me a safe space to be who I am becoming.

To my oldest daughter, Starr-Brianna, for her courage and quiet wisdom and for always encouraging me to keep going, but also to rest my mind and body.

To my son Antwan Jr. and my daughter Angel Skye, for surrounding me with so much love and support and giving me permission to be mom and for having so much high hopes for me and for expressing how proud you are of me.

Special Thanks

Special thanks to Linda Hewitt at Christian Faith Publishing for her encouraging words to remind me how important it was to finish the manuscript, To my publications specialist for coordinating the endless phases to book publication, to the editing and design team for taking the thoughts from my brain and making them come alive so you could have this very valuable book to read. To my dear friend Judge Tara Fentress, for her unselfish prayers and words of encouragement along this journey to the completion of this book, and to all my close friends who without knowing that I needed them, checked on me and encouraged me to keep going. Finally, to God almighty who I serve, for breathing life into this book as He used me as His humble servant to write these words of encouragement to a world in need.

Contents

Foreword

Insights about the author, my mother
By Starr-Brianna D. Wells

When I was asked to write the foreword for this book, I had chills, I smiled, and in my heart, I sang the words, "Of course." I know how long this book has been cooking up inside my mother, Dr. Dacia P. Hastings Proctor, and by the grace of God, she birthed this book. So as her daughter, there are no words to describe the infinite joy and nostalgia I feel to have the honor to call you "Mommy" and to see this book come to fruition.

The beauty and the electricity I feel in my veins for her makes me feel like I should bow at her feet with thanksgiving every time I'm in her presence and even when I am not. I had the opportunity to witness Dr. Dacia P. Hastings Proctor throughout many different changes and phases of her life. This may seem trivial, but it is an example of how Dr. Hastings Proctor has evolved.

One thing she and I would often giggle about is how much her choice of nail polish colors has changed today and is a contrast to the colors she wore when I was much younger and her only child. Somehow, she has evolved into a bolder and more confident woman, moving from wearing neutral warm tones like shades of pink and brown to bold colors like shades of turquoise blues and other colorful designs. Another change is when she found out she was pregnant with her second child, Antwan Jr., thirteen years after having me. His birth was immediately followed by her third, Angel Skye, fourteen months later. These two births and a new husband were not only big changes for her but also big changes for me, in a short space of time. The irony is, I had always prayed for a baby sister and brother, and after thirteen years, I had just about given up hope of ever having any biological ones.

God does have a sense of humor. Despite these changes, my mother persevered and had shown tremendous resiliency, which is why she is so qualified to write this book. She doesn't just share her clinical experiences; she puts her heart and soul into the practical examples and strategies, having gone through some new normal in her journey of life transitions.

This book has taught me that change is a continuum and will never cease. This is something we all subconsciously know, but this book will help you understand why it has been so challenging for you to confront your feelings and fears about change and uncertainty and offers helpful ways for you to recognize that you can work through every situation you may face in life by being open-minded, gaining skills in using the right tools and a whole lot of faith.

My mother is the smartest person I know. She has divine wisdom that only comes from God and the knowledge she has acquired during her time here on Earth. I recently read her high school yearbook, and it amazed me that everything she said she was going to do, she did. I would like the readers to know how diligently she worked to get this book done and how much she prayed and fasted and allowed God to literally give her the words to write in the very book you are holding right now. I remember she would say years ago, "God just gave me something for my book," and she'd write it in her notes until the time came that she'd begin writing the entire book.

These words you are about to read came straight from the heavens up above. It is appropriate for the times we are living in because so many people are struggling with stress, depression, anxiety, and other mental health challenges and are looking for hope and a way to cope in a world that at times seems to make very little sense.

If you've been struggling from coping with a significant incident that has occurred in your life or just can't see the end of a seemingly pitch-black tunnel, consider this book your guiding light. Allow this book to be the direction you have been quietly looking for and let it arm you with the tools you never knew you needed to propel you into your next.

Preface

Writing a book like this is no easy task. Most people expect a simple answer to how to deal with uncertainty, but just like the complex emotions we carry, understanding that we cannot control uncertainty can create a great deal of anxiety for some, creating a cycle of more questions and worry. There are times when it seems that no one understands, no one gets you, not even you. In those moments of emotional stirring and even distress, because the world seems to be moving way too fast to process your pain, process its many changes, or even fathom the myriad of frustrations you can face in a single day, just breathe. Breathing not only releases harmful toxins from the body but also brings the body to a state of calm and gives the mind the opportunity to function at its optimal level.

This book is a quick read and will serve as a reminder that you have everything you need inside you to be the best version of yourself even in a world that seems to have gone upside down and is showing no signs of ever going right side up. What remains to be true is that you might not have the power to fix the world, but you do have the power to see it through the lens of victory, believing that even you can survive in an upside-down world if you choose to see it right side up. Remember, the world is as it should be, and you get to choose how you react and respond to the world as it is.

Introduction

—Maya Angelou

There is so much good in this world for which we can be grateful. Yet gratitude can easily be overshadowed by fear, despair, grief and doubt, and if you add uncertainty to the mix, gratitude goes right out of the window. The novel coronavirus global pandemic has taught us so much about what it is like to live in an uncertain world. *Where were you when life as you knew it changed?*

Depending on who you are and what you remember about the global pandemic of 2019, your answers to that question may vary. However, if you are reading this book as a source of information and support to help you cope with the uncertainty you may be facing in your life today, your answers may also vary, whether or not you were around to experience the global pandemic firsthand or it was an event you read about or experienced through the eyes of someone else who lived through it. Regardless of who you are, and where you were, the coronavirus pandemic was an unforgettable and traumatic experience that will forever be etched in our minds. Therefore, it is important to look back with some self-reflection.

Think back. How did you feel when you witnessed the first images on your television screen of people around the world wearing face coverings? I remember thinking, *How strange.* This must be a part of a social experiment! Do you remember your immediate reaction when your part of the world went into lockdown? Did you understand what it would mean to be cut off from the outside world for an indefinite period? What did the restrictions on your life mean to you? Did the mixed messages you received ignite fear and wonder, or were you one who was simply living on edge waiting for further instructions? How did you feel knowing that you would have to work from home and your children would have to be schooled at home? Were you prepared or simply skating by the seat of your pants, looking to see what others were doing?

What about the impact of the long lines to get into grocery stores? Did it seem like an apocalypse where you lived noticing that supplies were running short, as evidenced by empty shelves? Were you in an area where you didn't have the freedom to shop on your terms but had to wait for your day of the week based on household name, size, or status?

How did it make you feel when you learned that people were dying in record numbers, and cases of outbreaks continued to rise as scientists scrambled to find ways to reduce the spread and decrease the death toll? Did you have confidence in the science? Or were you confused about what you would learn about the virus from day to day? Did your fear grow? What about trust? Did you find comfort in anything as it seemed that things grew even direr as the situation around the globe seem so volatile? When vaccinations were finally available, how did mixed messages make you feel? Who did you look to for answers? Did a vaccination offer you some sense of hope? Did you grow increasingly frustrated about the availability in your area of the world? Did the distribution/access illicit more emotions for you? What has it all been like for you?

Post pandemic, are things better or worse in your worldview? How are you coping with the mass shootings in schools places of worship, or any public place worldwide? Or the senseless acts of violence around the globe? Has the idea of fear and uncertainty turned to anger and rage in some? Have you been able to make sense of global uprisings, leadership takedowns, insurrections, lack of trust in world leaders, people being forced out of their homes, unstable society, and seemingly no safe place to exist? Are you confident about your tomorrow? Do human behaviors seem even more alarming than it has ever been? How about the rising costs? How have you been coping with the looming threat of a recession? Does things seem familiar, like we've-been-here-before? That the more things change, the more they stay the same? What about getting used to the "shrink-flation"—that is, paying more, but getting less at restaurants, in your packaged foods, at the grocery stores, and in just about every aspect of goods and services? Does it all seem so unfair, or simply to be expected by design?

Have unprecedented changes to laws and how things are done seemed like the world has been turned upside down? How are you adjusting to the new-world order? What about the many wars breaking out around the world? Have your thoughts been focused on the threats to the global economy, discrimination, divisiveness, and anger that continue to divide races and ethnic groups? Does it seem like the widespread disparities continue to worsen in this post pandemic world? How are you coping with all of it? Does it seem like the world is suffering from post-traumatic stress disorder (PTSD)?

So many questions and very few answers. Where can we find the answers to these important reflections? Do they exist? Is the world simply as it should be, or is it you who need to adjust the way you see and think of the world?

So much has changed in our world in a short space of time since the world was introduced to the global pandemic. Unprecedented changes often spark fear in those who experience them. The global pandemic was one major event, causing an increase in the world's level of anxiety! The reactions to fear of the unknown have shaken many to the core. Somehow, when major changes occur, we seem to forget that uncertainty has always been a part of the fabric of our lives. We somehow forget the emotions from the impact of change and the disruptions to our everyday norms.

When change occurs, it is normal to react like we are experiencing it for the first time in our lives. We often personalize change and might even say, "Why is this happening to me?" Some people cringe and resist a disruption to the status quo, yet change is an inevitable reality of life. If you have lived long enough, chances are you have been through so many change events in your life. Change is inevitable! Change can seem hard, depending on the level and size of the change. This is the main reason we face change by trying to avoid it, resist it, or run away from it. Yet it is one of those things in life you will never be able to outrun. Without change, you would not be where you are today.

The present world we live in is choking with the fear of an uncertain tomorrow. Yet when has tomorrow ever offered some sense of certainty? People are operating from a place of anxiety, too afraid to remember the simple steps to achieve calm; stop, pause, and breathe. The world seems to be on edge, braced for what might be next. If you are reading this introduction, you are probably hoping to get mentally prepared for the *next*. If so, you are on the right track because there will be a *next*. What that next will look like remains to be seen.

How you react and respond to the crucibles in your life depends on you, your mindset, and your level of preparation for how you think about change and how you choose to behave in an inevitably changing and evolving world order, sometimes bringing with it tough stuff with which to cope. The good news is that this book offers seven practical tips for coping emotionally in an uncertain world. As we embrace what has become our "new normal," in this life after the global pandemic, you may need to give yourself permission to return to the basics of how to adapt to change, manage emotions and reactions, and accept the things of which you do not and will not have control.

The purpose of this book is to provide you with seven practical tips that will serve as reminders to help you cope emotionally with uncertainty. These tips will allow you to change the way you view the world and understand your place and purpose in a world that is ever changing and will continue to change in unimaginable ways. At the end of every change event, remember the world is as it is and as it should be. May your hearts and minds be open as you read this book.

A Prayer for Faith, Strength, Encouragement, and an Open Mind

Heavenly Father,

We live in troublesome times. It is hard to wrap our minds around the events that continue to overwhelm our existence, creating mass fear and despair within us. Help us to stand courageous and anchor our belief in You, now more than ever before. Help us to learn to trust in You despite all that we must face and will continue to face as we journey through this life. Help us to remember that we may not have the power to change the world, but we do have the power to change the way we view the world by seeing our world through the eyes of faith, hope, and love. May this book be a resource to remind us that we have everything we need inside us to cope in a world that at times makes no sense to us. Allow us to be reminded that the same power that lives in You lives inside of all of us because we are Yours and have been made in Your image and likeness. It is not Your intention for us to suffer, but that suffering is a part of life. But we can hope in Your promise to always see us through. Help us not to forget that we were made to be resilient, and with your power and strength, we can conquer every obstacle and battle we face. This is my prayer in Your name.
Amen.

> Do not let your hearts be troubled. You believe in God; believe also in me. My Father's house has many rooms; if that were not so, would I have told you that I am going there to prepare a place for you? And if I go and prepare a place for you, I will come back and take you to be with me that you also may be where I am. You know the way to the place where I am going. (John 14:1–4 NIV)

Chapter 1

Change Your Mindset

And now, dear brothers and sisters, one final thing. Fix your thoughts on what is true, and honorable, and right, and pure, and lovely, and admirable. Think about things that are excellent and worthy of praise.

—Philippians 4:8 (NLT)

If you change the way you look at things, the things you look at change.

—Wayne Dyer

Uncertainty is a normal part of life, yet for some people, it can be the most troubling and upsetting part of life. The stress of uncertainty may leave you feeling a sense of hopelessness, fear, helplessness, frustration, worry, depression, and anxiety. Change may even leave you feeling stuck and less confident. These feelings can have a negative impact on our lives and impact how we cope. Uncertainty can leave some of us stuck with spiraling thoughts of *what ifs*.

I remember counseling many people in the early phases of the pandemic. The most common reaction to the pandemic was *fear*. It didn't help that there were mixed messages channeled from various media sources that you probably did not know who to trust or what to believe. As people continued to live their lives in fear from day to day not knowing what tomorrow would bring, anxiety replaced fear; and eventually, for some, depression was added to the anxiety. We watched the political battles, civil unrest, economic downturn, and increase in hate and intolerance, for differences emerged at catastrophic levels. We watched as the world seemed to unravel at the seams and explode from within, as so many mixed emotions fueled unprecedented reactions. It almost seemed as if we had returned to a reality of ancient times—all from a pandemic that knew no boundaries beyond race, ethnicity, gender, age, socioeconomic status.

Thoughts from fear can seem like a dark, powerful force. It overtakes the mind, and if you give fear a home inside your mind, it seems to take on a life of its own. Proverbs 23:7 reads, "As a man thinketh so is he." This truth has been expressed in many literary, artistic, and poetic areas of life. Even philosophical thinkers such as Marcus Aurelius Antoninus echo the proverbs about the thoughts that exist in our minds and how our lives become what we think and where we focus. It might be relevant to insert Aurelius as one example of the origins of thought examination. He is one philosophical thinker who has been largely quoted for his conclusions about how we become what we think. Aurelius knew his fair share of uncertainty and despair as he faced many trials such as the death of his wife and children, who died one by one, and even the uncertainty of his reign, and the wars he led during his time (Aurelius et al. 1908).

One might conclude that it is hard to change your mindset when you face trials of proportionate size. Some might even say, "I am not like other people," or, "I don't have the same resources as you." Some believe that people with resources have the skills to change their mindset and move through times of adversity with greater strength and resilience than do others because they were taught those *skills*. Those may be fair arguments, but the one thing that mentally healthy beings have in common is that they know how to use the "power of thought." With the power of thought, you can choose to control the way you think.

The mind works in a methodical way. We think thoughts that then lead to our feelings. When we choose feelings based on our thoughts, those feelings will ultimately lead to a reaction. When you feel anxious, it is because you are thinking anxious thoughts. Here's an illustration of what that might look like. I once worked with a female patient. We will call her Daniella. Daniella struggled with anxiety most of her life. Daniella was deeply troubled by not being able to know what tomorrow had in store for her. She proclaimed to believe in God and admitted to knowing the word of God. But she said she just had to know if she would ever be in a lasting relationship, marry, and have children. The idea of watching her friends get married and have children was hard for her. Relationships triggered her fears, which led to anxiety. Relationships became her trigger after she had experienced so many failures in her past relationships.

> You cannot change what will be, but you can change the way you think about what *is* and *will be*.

Although quite young and every other area in her life was going well, she lived anxiously with the idea that something was wrong with her because she wasn't in a relationship or couldn't even keep one. The more she thought about something being wrong with her, the more she believed she could quite possibly be flawed. She had given up on any possibility of a satisfying relationship. No matter how hard she tried, Daniella could not bring her thoughts to focus on the present and focus on what she did have in front of her. The thing that she wanted, but didn't have in her life now, to her meant that she would never have it. Daniella had literally charted the course of her future with relationships because of her thinking. Consequently, her way of thinking overshadowed every other area of success in her life.

When an uncertain situation hits you at the core, the most powerful weapon you have is to change the way you think about that situation. The natural reaction will always be to try to control uncertainty, fix it, or try to find a solution, but that is simply fighting a losing battle. No one can fully predict nor control what will happen tomorrow. Having the ability to say to yourself, "I cannot change what will be, but I can change the way I think about what will be," is powerful! Thus, the first tip is to *"change your mindset."*

Through our work together and Daniella deciding to change her focus, she realized that even after getting the very thing she thought would calm her worries, she just found something else to worry about. She even worried when things were going too well. Ultimately, even after getting the coveted relationship she desired and thought would complete her life, she couldn't rest on what she had received, and eventually sabotaged her relationship.

The way you think will lead to a set of feelings, and the way you feel will lead to your reactions or outcomes (Beck 1995). For example, "I will never be able to pass this exam." What will then follow are feelings of anxiety, self-defeat, and maybe even sadness and depression. The more you think that thought, the more you eventually will feel those feelings, leading to a reaction of nervousness, lack of self-confidence, or second-guessing your answers on the test. Ultimately, even what you know or had studied will not matter because your mindset will cause you to fail the exam, thus validating the thought you had in mind.

Similarly, during the first year of the pandemic, even after restrictions of the lockdown were lifted, I had some patients who still could not leave their homes. They were so riddled with fear and had become conditioned to the thoughts of fear, that they held on to the safety nets they had established within their homes. For many of them, leaving home would mean they would, in fact, contract COVID-19. The thoughts of contracting COVID-19 and what could happen to them was so etched in their minds that they developed an unhealthy fear of leaving their home. They had become so accustomed to the conditioning they developed in their mindset about leaving home that lockdown had become their norm.

> Your perception of things becomes the reality you adopt.

Adjusting your thinking may not be your default. In fact, it is one of the hardest things to do, especially when you believe that your negative thoughts are based in reality. In other words, your perception of things becomes the reality you adopt. When your perception of reality is skewed, other negative influences can easily become the strongest voice you hear. These can come in the form of other people such as coworkers, friends, or family members. The slightest validation of your thoughts from other people's skewed reality becomes the fuel that you need to add to your already-spiraling thoughts. Someone else may share something that happened to them or someone they knew, and suddenly, that something also happened to you.

Another strong form of influence is the media. Our lives are heavily saturated by media sources of various kinds. We get instant news from our smart devices, social media feed, or traditional evening news or newspaper. Even when you may not want it, someone might package the news in an email or text message and share it with you. It is a good idea to stay abreast of what is happening around you, but too much of anything is not always good for you. Allowing media sources to infiltrate your thinking can keep you living in fear and riddled with anxiety. You see bad news sells, and it sells big. But bad news has a way of keeping your mindset in the red zone of fear—especially if you are not skilled at managing your thoughts.

You can control how much of the external influences you allow into your thought life. Simple things like turning off notifications, discriminating about your news source and how much you take in on a daily or weekly basis, and watching who you talk to and when, are all practical ways to aid in changing and managing what you focus on. Many people keep the news going around the clock twenty-four hours, seven days a week. They wonder why they can't escape the cycle of negative and fearful thinking. Still, others spend too much time with negative and anxious people who allow their emotions to rule their actions. What they think about, becomes what you ultimately think about because the influence is so strong. You get into a cycle where you can't tell the difference between their truth and your reality. Ultimately, you should avoid allowing negative sources to influence your thoughts. You can simply step away and create healthy boundaries to protect your mindset.

Another helpful strategy is bringing to your remembrance a time when you overcame the emotions caused by difficult situations such as a loss, divorce, or some life-changing event. The idea of reaching back helps you tap into your resiliency and reminds the brain that it can think hopeful and optimistic thoughts. Changing your mindset means challenging your need to have certainty and control over the unknown.

A patient I've worked with struggles with control. She has difficulty letting go of the things she can't control. She shared how her family played a trick on her one day while planning a party for a special event. She was given very little information about attending the party. She was told to get dressed and show up. All week leading up to the party, she struggled with not knowing the details of the event. She had even tried to get other people to share what they knew about the party and venue. No one shared any information leaving her to plan and prepare for the party, uncertain about where it was going to be and what she should wear.

For many of you, that may be a nerve-wracking thought. But how many times have you just allowed things to be what they are and to go with the flow? My patient was forced to do this, and although anxious about what the outcome might be, she went along with it. In the end, she realized that things worked out regardless of how she felt about "not knowing" the details. She also taught herself a valuable skill that sometimes you must just let go and go with the flow. This is a valuable skill that her brain will remember.

Another very important principle to adopt when shifting your mindset is to recognize and tap into your resilience and strength. When we are going through a difficult time, it is hard to imagine anything else and how we will ever get through the difficulty. Your thoughts will tell you that you will never get through this and that this is the worst thing that has ever happened to you. You then become reactive to those thoughts, forcing yourself to isolate or withdraw, become depressed, or lack hope. However, you should understand that there is nothing new under the sun.

A powerful yet practical biblical expression is found in Ecclesiastes 1:9 (NLT), "History merely repeats itself. It has all been done before. Nothing under the sun is truly new." If you adopt this principle, you will understand that you can allow your mind to bring you back to a space and place in time where you faced a certain difficulty or situation. Yet the fact that you are here today should be a testament to the strength and resilience you have within. When you realize that, you can hone those strengths by shifting your thinking; and by tapping into your inner strengths, you can be motivated to believe that you can and will get through your difficult circumstance because you have been able to do so before. Allow yourself to stop and think about what it was like to go through a previous challenge or situation and how you made it through. For some, it may be allowing enough time, for others, prayer and support, or a combination of multiple things. Whatever it was for you, it still works here.

Your need to control uncertainty is a state of mind that will keep you in a space of always fighting against time. No one can control time. Therefore, no one has the power to control tomorrow. We may spend time making predictions, and in some cases, our forecasts based on careful calculations and probabilities may seem accurate, but in the grand scheme of things, we cannot be certain about tomorrow. When you try to control uncertainty, you must challenge your thinking around uncertainty. What does it mean to you to need to control the things of which you do not have control? In fact, trying to control an uncertain tomorrow is wasted energy and time. Instead, you should focus on that which you have and always will have control of, and that is how you choose to react and respond to situations around you.

> You could miss the present moment because you are too busy managing tomorrow.

When you master your ability to challenge your thinking, responses, and reactions, your situations and circumstances will look different. Remember, choosing the way you think about things requires a change in your thinking, and ultimately, you will be able to change the situation around you because you changed the way you viewed it. One thing to think about in challenging your need to control uncertainty is what you could miss in the present moment because you are too busy managing tomorrow.

How has your state of mind helped or hurt you in coping with uncertainty? Depending on the situation, your state of mind can impact how you cope and dictate whether you stay stuck or immobilized by fear and defeat. Fear of the unknown is often immobilizing and can keep you from realizing your true potential. The first step in changing your mindset is being aware of how you think or what you are thinking about.

If you are one who commonly harbors negative, self-defeating thoughts, always predicting the worst, then you need to challenge those thoughts to change the way you think. This is known as "cognitive restructuring" (Ellis 2001). Our brains can be molded and restructured to unlearn patterns of thinking. Unhealthy patterns of thinking can keep you in a defeatist state where you choose negative, rigid thoughts as opposed to flexible thoughts, which can and will lead to more favorable outcomes.

A helpful strategy is using the worst, best, likely, technique (Beck 2021) to train your brain to focus on the most likely outcome. Cognitive distortions, according to Beck, can be changed through a process called "cognitive restructuring," which is to change the way you think by challenging your beliefs or adjusting unhelpful ways of thinking (Beck 2021). Consider this example. You have an upcoming presentation, but you are very nervous about presenting because your audience will consist of what you perceive to be some very important people. The thoughts you believe to be true and predict to happen is "I am going to mess up this presentation, everyone will think that I am incompetent, and I will lose my credibility." That thought is called, "predicting the worst," and is not the likely thing to happen, but you perceive it to be. Nevertheless, harboring that thinking can lead to unfavorable outcomes because of your anxious thinking. To change your thinking, you must challenge your thoughts and beliefs, and ask yourself, is that the likely thing that could happen here? Perhaps not. The likely thing, which might be the best, is that you get through the presentation, and everyone applauds because you did a great job, or you get through the presentation and received feedback that you can incorporate into your presentation the next time around, which is the "likely" case scenario.

Another great self-coaching journaling activity that can help you restructure your negative thinking pattern might look like this.

Step 1: Write down your negative thoughts daily.
Example: "No one likes me," "I don't have any friends," or "No one ever calls or invites me out."
Step 2: Analyze your thoughts by examining each thought, the circumstances surrounding those thoughts, the time of day, and your mood.
Analysis: "It is Friday night," I am home alone," "My phone hasn't wrung," "I haven't received a text message," or "I feel sad and lonely."
Step 3: Determine if your thoughts are grounded in facts. In other words, how do you know that your thoughts are true? If your thoughts are true, how can you think about them differently? If they are not true, challenge yourself to change your thoughts to more realistic, factual thoughts or let go of the negative thoughts.
Challenge the lie: "Last week, I went out with a group of friends after work. My coworkers always invite me to go out after work or to go to lunch. Last month, I heard from an old college friend who told me he's been thinking about me and misses all the fun we used to have."
Flexible thinking/options: The next time I feel sad and lonely, I can choose to make plans with coworkers or schedule coffee dates with old friends to catch up.
Step 4: For every negative thought, counter those thoughts with at least three positive ones.
Negative thought: "No one likes me."
Change negative thoughts: "My family loves me." "My friends say I am fun to be around." "My neighbor is always asking me to come over for dinner."
Positive thoughts: "My coworkers tell me how much they appreciate my teamwork."

People often think that when they choose positivity, it means denying what they feel. Some might even call positivity "fake thinking." I have heard this all too often. That's the furthest thought from the truth. In fact, choosing positivity means you acknowledge your truth, your thoughts, and everything you feel. With that acknowledgment, you are then able to decide to choose to think about your situation from a standpoint that can help you get you through a tough situation instead of a standpoint that will keep you stuck in your circumstances—either searching for a way out or searching for a way to cope.

Changing your mindset requires a commitment to improving the way your mind works and consistent practice and patience with the process. The more you practice, the more you will grow your thought awareness, allowing

> Mind maintenance will always be necessary because of life's uncertainty.

you to choose more helpful thoughts instead of self-defeating ones. As you become better at choosing your thoughts, it will also become necessary to develop strategies to better manage your thoughts. Your thought maintenance strategy might include limiting your exposure to external factors that might influence your thoughts such as the media, unhealthy social situations, and toxic people. Recognize that mind maintenance will always be necessary because of the uncertainty life brings.

Chapter 1 Application: Change Your Mindset

1. Changing your mindset requires daily intention and commitment to the process. How can you use the methods described in chapter 1 to commit to changing negative thinking patterns? Jot down your brainstorm ideas for your process of change.

    ____

    ____

    ____

    ____

    ____

2. How can you challenge your thinking when negative or fearful thoughts enter your mind?

    ____

    ____

    ____

    ____

    ____

3. Jot down your awareness about your thinking patterns. For example, "I often default to negative thinking, or I often predict that people are talking about me in a negative way."

    ____

    ____

    ____

    ____

    ____

4. Are these thoughts based in reality?

    ____

    ____

    ____

    ____

5. What evidence do you have that your thoughts are realistic?

    ____

    ____

    ____

    ____

    ____

6. What evidence do you have that your thoughts are unrealistic?

    ____

    ____

    ____

    ____

    ____

7. If your thoughts are realistic, identify at least three options that
    you can explore as solutions to your concerns or situation.

    ____

    ____

    ____

    ____

    ____

8. If your thoughts are not based on facts or reality, consider letting
    them go. What are three ways you can abandon your unrealis-
    tic thoughts? For example: *Write the thought on a piece of paper
    and burn it. Say to those thoughts, "You are not in control of my
    thinking. You are not reality based, so I am choosing to let you go
    for good."*

    ____

    ____

    ____

    ____

    ____

9. How can you use the technique "worst, best, likely, to apply to your current circumstance or to situations that you might be dealing with?

____

____

____

____

____

10. What are three to five positive thoughts I can use to counter my negative way of thinking about my situation or circumstance?

____

____

____

____

____

Repeat this process as many times as you need to. Initially, you may need to do this using pen and paper every time you find yourself in an anxious cycle. Eventually, you will be able to do this as your default method and thwart negative thoughts as quickly as they come. Remember, changing the way you think requires time and commitment to the process as it involves a commitment to changing the way your brain works as it relates to the thought console of your brain. Keep a record of your process to track your progress along the way.

Key Chapter Take-Aways

1. You become what you think about or choose to focus on.
2. You have the power to control your thoughts.
3. If you do the work and remain consistent, you can manage your thoughts.
4. Thought maintenance is necessary to remain successful at thought management.

A Prayer for Your Thought Life

Heavenly Father,

Teach me how to keep an open mind and think with flexible thoughts. Help me to remember that the thoughts You have for me are for good and that I can choose only to think about those things that are for my good and that will yield good fruits and good outcomes. Please remind me that when I am tempted to think thoughts that are not based on Your promises or Your truth for my life, I have the power to change those thoughts to ones that are positive, restorative, and uplifting. Help me to be consistent in my practice of changing my mindset and become skilled in mastering my thought life. This is my prayer in Your name.
Amen.

Chapter 2

Manage Your Emotions

For God gave us a spirit not of fear, but of power, love, and self-control.

—2 Timothy 1:7 (ESV)

*Your emotions are slave to your thoughts, and
you are slave to your emotions.*

—Anonymous

The global pandemic has impacted the world politically, economically, socially, behaviorally, racially, mentally, physically, and overall—emotionally. People have made so many emotional decisions leading to increased rates of suicide, increased divorce and separations, permanent business closures, decisions to leave jobs, decisions to leave their homes, mass shootings at alarming rates, and some have even made decisions that are politically and racially charged. The world looks a lot different today than it did prior to the coronavirus pandemic. Our thoughts have also changed drastically, and so have our behaviors.

It appears that the world is suffering from post-traumatic stress disorder (PTSD), a condition often fueled by a past traumatic incident that the brain remembers and causes a reaction when there is a present threat or similar situation. Let's take a moment for introspection. What were your thoughts and behaviors like pre-pandemic? How have they shifted post pandemic? What are the things you've missed prepandemic that are no longer present or have been altered in this post pandemic world? How do those changes make you feel?

To some, things seem to be back to some sense of normal, albeit a "new normal." It makes me wonder, *Did the world forget about 2020?* Fear of dying seemed to bring out the kindness and compassion in some while others displayed even more anger, callousness, and lack of control. It seems today that more of our fears and frustrations have transitioned to anger, rage, and even, in some cases, lack of regard for others. Still, others seem numb, just moving through life with little regard for precautions or safety. The scripture, 2 Timothy 3:2 (NIV) reminds us that "people will be lovers of themselves, lovers of money, boastful, proud, abusive, disobedient to their parents, ungrateful, unholy." We are living in these predicted times. This also tells me that what we feel today, we will not feel tomorrow because our emotions are fickle. Those who allow them to rule become enslaved by them, resulting in people making decisions that are emotionally charged and often regretted.

> Emotions move with ebbs and flows, just as our thoughts change from moment to moment.

Emotions move with ebbs and flows, just as our thoughts change from moment to moment. One moment you may be feeling great, snapping your fingers and bopping your head to your favorite tune while the next moment, you receive some disturbing news that instantly changes your mood. Situations and circumstances around us often seem to have the power to change our emotions. Yet did you know that the emotions you experience are a choice?

How many times have you felt a certain way but couldn't quite identify what you were feeling? We have many emotions available at our disposal, but we are not always able to identify what we are feeling and sometimes why we are feeling what we feel. Some of us have difficulty connecting our emotions to our thoughts or intellect. In fact, we feel emotions before truly being able to verbalize what we are feeling. Sometimes you may feel an emotion, but it may take some time before you can give it a name or label. The ability to identify or pinpoint your emotions depends largely on self-awareness, a characteristic of our emotional intelligence, commonly known as EQ.

Emotional intelligence (EQ) means having the ability to be in tune with your emotions and identify what they are, while being able to have an awareness and concern about the emotions of others, which is social awareness. (Goleman 1995). Emotionally intelligent people are often much better at verbally expressing or communicating emotions than those who are not. This is because they have self-awareness.

For example, an emotionally intelligent person may be able to say to someone, "I feel sad because what you just said hurt my feelings," whereas someone who lacks emotional intelligence may feel the feelings of sadness, but instead of expressing sadness, may shut down or display sadness because he or she may not be able to appropriately communicate the emotion of sadness.

Self-awareness is a skill where you can connect the dots between your feelings, thoughts, and actions and how those feelings and actions may be impacting those around you or how others may be feeling and behaving in relation to their interaction with you. Therefore, to be able to manage your emotions, you must first be aware of them. When you are aware of them, you can then identify them, communicate them, and manage what you feel because your emotions are your own.

Emotional intelligence is a skill that also requires effective communication, observation, and listening. Daniel Goleman, author of *Emotional Intelligence: Why It Can Matter More than IQ*, believes "emotional self-awareness is the building block of the next fundamental emotional intelligence: being able to shake off a bad mood." During times of uncertainty, our emotions can be very unstable. This is because of fear and our perception that we may be facing a situation that we cannot control.

Whether your perception of your circumstances is real or imagined, because of fear, you may experience a myriad of different emotions related to that situation. This might be based on the experiences you may have had in your life, experiences dealing with the unknown, or something that might threaten what you know the outcome could be. The mind will try to protect you by forcing you to think of ways to see the outcome. Unfortunately, often, most people will default to the negative, thus triggering more negative emotions.

One of my patients, who we'll call Dan, had a difficult time communicating his fear of becoming a father although rationally, his desire was to father children with his wife. He had had a difficult relationship with his father growing up, and as an adult, his current relationship with his father was estranged. Dan's mind would not let him feel and express the fears he had; perhaps they are fears of failing at fatherhood or becoming just like his own father, with whom he still had issues to resolve.

Instead of expressing his fears to his wife, Dan used one of the dangerous things that humans do to protect their emotions—he ran. His running translated into internet porn, which he eventually acted upon. This led to devastating consequences almost costing him his marriage. Seeking help from a professional helped Dan to connect the dots leading back to his own emotions of fears that linked to unresolved issues with his own father.

A good way to look at emotions in a situation of uncertainty is to examine a well-known event that occurred in history that received national attention all around the world. Recall the true events of the thirty-three Chilean coal miners who were trapped underground in a coal mine in Chile for sixty-nine days (Tobar 2014). I imagine the miners went to work that day like any other ordinary day, kissed their loved ones goodbye, and not knowing what would take place in their lives hours later. I imagine they laughed and talked with one another as they worked like any other ordinary day. I also imagine their loved ones expected them to return home at the end of their work day. But later that day, an unprecedented event was coming unbeknown to the miners.

Accounts of the story tell us that one large stone that fell through the mine from a nearby mountain set off a chain reaction, trapping the thirty-three miners deep within the cave mine where they were working (Tobar 2014). Imagine the fear the miners must have felt as they scrambled to collect themselves physically and mentally trying to figure out what just happened. I imagine they may have called out to one another to see if anyone had survived the unexpected crash that now had them trapped in the mine.

The emotions were probably running high as the hours went by as they tried to free themselves from the entrapment. Perhaps as hours turned into days, they began to lose hope. Perhaps they worried about their family members who were now wondering about the fate of their loved ones after they didn't make it home. The miners, their loved ones, and those hearing the news were all likely dealing with a myriad of emotions, some of which may have included sadness, worry, and fear often brought on by uncertainty.

After many rescue efforts, one would think that hope on the outside of the mine grew dim. Yet what kept those thirty-three miners alive after sixty-nine days was their hope, faith, and the encouragement they shared with one another. This was also true for the miners' family members who were waiting outside the mine at what was called "Camp Hope." According to witnesses, the miner's loved ones never lost hope that their loved ones would make it out of the ruins of the mine safely and alive.

> Harboring negative emotions only makes you emotionally and physically sick.

What do this story and Dan's situation teach us about managing our emotions in times of uncertainty? Consider this. It takes more energy to be upset and sad, and those emotions does not yield any good fruit. In fact, harboring negative emotions only makes us emotionally and physically sick, drained, and unable to employ flexible thinking.

When we are in a state of emotional drain, what good can we be to ourselves and others? How can we look for options and hope for the best outcome in our situation? Standing firm to our hope as the miners and their loved ones did is what helped them to reach the favorable outcome that day when thirty-three miners emerged from deep within the mines and had story after story of hope and faith to share with those in waiting.

Perhaps you might expect that the emotions of those who were trapped in the mountains would be far dimmer, than those waiting on the outside to see what would happen next, but the common word that threads both the trapped miners and their loved ones waiting above ground was *hope*. In fact, you may be thinking at this moment, *What if I hold out hope but the worst still happens?* That's the thing about uncertainty; you never quite know what you will get. However, what you should know is you can manage the emotions you have about uncertainty. What is also true is that what you get depends on you. You have two ways of looking at it: If you are waiting in anticipation of an outcome, but you are deeply mired in fear, sadness, and despair, the outcome is harder to deal with because of your emotional state of being. However, if you have maintained an attitude of hope and joy even amid your uncertainty, you are more likely to cope and deal with an outcome even if it is perceived as unfavorable because of the attitude you maintained.

Even Dan's story also has a somewhat happy ending, depending on how you look at it. After months of painful processing of emotions in both marriage and individual counseling, Dan's wife was able to forgive him, and Dan was able to make connections about his behaviors and link them to his fears and other emotions connected to feelings of inadequacy and unresolved issues with his father.

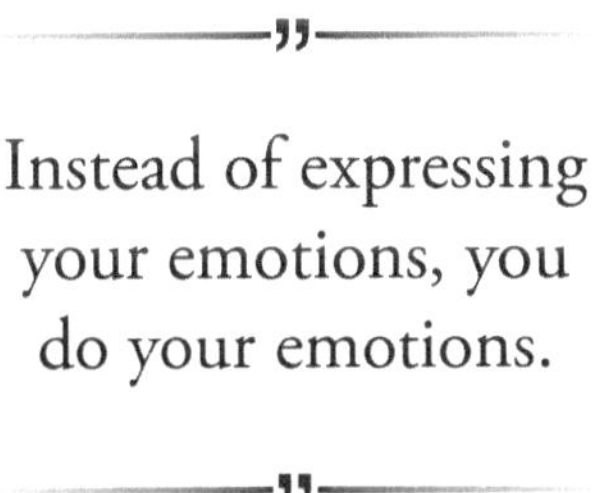

Instead of expressing your emotions, you do your emotions.

All emotions are valid. That is why we have them. They are designed to help us be expressive and cry out whether in sadness, happiness, or disappointment. Yet although all emotions are valid, some emotions are not looked upon favorably simply because most of you have not learned how to appropriately communicate negative emotions. Instead of expressing our emotions, we do our emotions. In other words, for some of you, it may be hard to tell someone else that what they did cause you to feel angry, frustrated, or disappointed. There is nothing wrong with expressing those words. Yet the angry emotion can be looked upon unfavorably because instead of saying you are angry, you might resort to breaking things, using profanities, or using other intimidating tactics to get your point across. Behaving in this manner doesn't really communicate or convey what you really want to say. Instead, people read the emotions and miss the unspoken message.

The pandemic seemed to unearth a great deal of anger and sadness in many people. It seemed that people are either imploding (i.e., turning their emotions inward) or exploding (i.e., turning their emotions outward). Fear makes these emotions worse and seems to mute people from really expressing to one another what they are feeling in healthy ways. Unfortunately, civil unrest has grown at epic proportions worldwide, divorce rates increasing, destruction of self and property, taking the lives of others because of hate and intolerance, violence of every imaginable kind, senseless war and war crimes, and mass shootings worldwide taking innocent lives—all driven by unmanaged emotions. Unexpressed emotions need to be processed and communicated appropriately. Have you ever found that even when people don't understand your emotions, getting them out takes away at least 50 percent of the pent-up emotions? You can even begin to feel physically calm after airing how you feel.

You may be thinking, *There's no excuse for these behaviors we have witnessed all over the world.* We have numerous outlets to help people learn how to appropriately express their emotions to avoid dire consequences. That may be true in your mind. However, the connection is not always apparent. Most people take the easier, most impulsive way out to express what they feel because it is more convenient to have a knee-jerk reaction or feed the flesh than it is to pause and process before acting.

Ephesians 4:31 (NIV) reads "Get rid of all bitterness, rage, and anger, brawling, and slander, along with every form of malice." Although controlling our emotions is explicitly stated in the Bible and in numerous pieces of literature available as resources, many people still have a difficult time managing their emotions. Unfortunately, it is what makes the world such a difficult place to navigate at times. Most people prefer to feed the flesh because it is momentary satisfaction.

But momentary satisfaction at times can lead to lifelong consequences. This is where the process of taking action begins—in the mind.

You have a thought, and if that thought is negative, negative emotions will follow; and the longer you dwell on the negative emotions, the more likely you will choose your default actions. Your default actions tend to be those actions you learned early on in life—whether to yell and scream at the top of your lungs to get your point across or shut down and isolate to hopefully communicate your point. Ultimately, no one really hears or understands the message, sometimes not even you.

So how do I manage my emotions when other people's emotions are influencing my emotions? Is it possible to feel and take on the emotions of others around me? At times, we have stress in our lives because of loved ones, or those closely connected to us may display emotions and behaviors that may get to us and at times even get inside of us. The challenge may be because of the emotions of someone living right in your home where every day watching them struggle with their emotions is draining because some of the other person's emotions may get projected onto you and leave you questioning, "Is it me, or is it them?"

> Our emotions are our own; we choose them, and therefore, we must own them.

It may be someone who you have an intimate relationship with or someone who you work and have to interact with every day. These circumstances are the hardest because you may feel like wherever you go, there they are. When you find yourself in a toxic cycle where the people around you or in society cause you to take on similar emotions, you must recognize that it is your responsibility to learn how to not let other people's stuff get inside you. You may ask, What if it is my spouse, my child, my family members, or even my boss? Again, our emotions are our own; we choose them, and therefore, we must own them.

When other people are mad, upset, or have a meltdown, it doesn't mean that you must in turn become mad, upset, or display a meltdown. When you do so, you have given over control of your emotions to something or someone else. Thus, you have rendered yourself powerless over your emotions. That situation, circumstance, or person now has you in the palm of their hands like a puppet on a string, forcing you to feel what they feel and behave the way they are behaving.

Take back your control, keep your cool, and choose your emotions in these situations. When someone else feels down, empathize with them, ask them if there is anything you can do, but realize that you don't have to lose a perfectly good day because someone else chooses to be upset or say mean and harsh things. Choose the emotions you want to feel and keep your emotional power.

Emotional distress can also be caused by fears of rejection, which can be gripping and can lead to ideas of self-blame and lack of self-worth. This happened to my patient who we will call Kai. Kai never knew her biological father, and the one time she tried to contact him through a letter, he rejected her. What was worse, her mother never wanted to talk about her biological father, so Kai always felt unloved. As a teenager, she felt her mother's indifference toward her. As a middle-aged adult, trying to piece her life together, Kai set out on her own to find her father again. Still traumatized by the memories of the earlier experiences of rejection, she feared it would happen again. She lived with feelings of rejection for many years even in her own marriage. The rejection became a lack of self-worth, which led to self-blame for everything else that happened in her life.

Kai never felt worthy and couldn't accept genuine love. As a result, she was faced with more rejection in her life which further perpetuated her thoughts about herself. Kai learned how to see her existence through damaged lenses often feeling taken advantage of yet making allowances for other people and giving others permission to treat her poorly. Kai eventually wrote her father a letter after finding his last known address. While she waited, she was filled with anxiety.

Living with this kind of uncertainty can be gripping leaving you feeling as if your destiny is controlled by your emotions. Waiting in anticipation can fuel increased anxiety and without the appropriate tools to help you self-regulate, you may impulsively act on your emotions as we learned from Dan's story earlier in the chapter.

Kai experienced a flood of emotions not knowing how her father would respond to her contacting him or if he could or would respond and be open to a relationship with her. But let me ask you this, even when you choose to go on an emotional roller coaster with worry, fear, anger, sadness, uncertainty, or whatever else you might feel in a similar situation, would any of those emotions change the outcome? That answer is a resounding no. Harboring a flood of negative emotions can leave you feeling worse than ever and can lead to dire consequences for your emotional and physical health. Negative emotions have negative consequences! So now you not only have the problem you started with, but you also have added at least one or two others because of choosing to hold on to negative thoughts.

The Bible says in Proverbs 3:5–6, "Trust in the Lord with all your heart and lean not your own understanding. In all your ways acknowledge Him and He will direct your path." This is a powerful verse to memorize to remind you that there are things you cannot and shouldn't try to control or even comprehend. A patient whom we will call Jennifer struggled with infertility. The idea that her thought process was that she controlled her life was something she was taught growing up. What she learned as a child was reinforced by the outcomes she always expected and got. She had the idea that whatever she wanted she could get it because she controlled the outcome she expected and ultimately the way her life turned out. The shock of not being able to control when she conceived was shocking. What was even more disturbing was the family unit she expected, i.e. a family of four, was a disappointing reality when it didn't happen on her terms. This disappointment led her to question her thinking and everything she grew up believing about the outcome of her life. She became moody, irritable, depressed, and obsessed with trying to control the very thing she couldn't control. Acknowledging what is in front of you, and choosing to hope for the outcome you want can lead you to choose more positive emotions that give you far better outcomes for your emotional and physical health. You simply know when you know, and a favorable outcome is always the bonus prize! This is what Jennifer needed to come to terms with and accept to address her cognitive distortions which were ingrained in her thought processes based on how she was raised to think.

Kai and Jennifer are no different from many of you who face adversities in your life and then turn your emotions inward thinking you will never be good enough. Managing spiraling emotions can be difficult. However, there are simple steps you can take to manage emotions of any kind, especially negative ones. Unfortunately, if you don't learn how to manage your emotions, they will manage you and can and will spill over and entangle themselves in other parts of your life. For some, it could take years of working through the pain of trauma with a trained professional before you can handle or manage everyday emotions in practical ways. However, one strategy often thought to be useful for helping people process emotions first before taking action is using your "instead of." The technique is quite simple but requires commitment and practice. Conceptually, it is simple. Emotionally, it is not as easy to restructure your thinking so that the technique becomes your default, especially if you are not used to processing emotions in this manner. We will examine the concept in a moment. Let's use a sequence of desires, emotions, pauses, and actions.

> Manage your emotions before they manage you.

We all have desires that may be classified as physiological or psychological. Unfortunately, we are not always able to understand or express those desires because we are not in touch with ourselves and our emotions. Your desires, fueled by thought, will lead to emotions such as sadness, fear, anger, and pain, whether you are aware of the emotions or not. For example, some people turned to substances to deal with their frustrations, sadness, fears, and despair, especially during the Coronavirus pandemic lockdown. Unfortunately, using substances to cope only leads to more problems. Substances have never been able to solve a problem, but abuse or misuse of substances leads to more problems that are physical, emotional, and even social. Substances such as drugs and alcohol are highly addictive and mask a situation you are dealing with, creating a façade of a resolution to your problem; but psychologically, there still exists underlying pain, anger, and frustration from the problem you began with.

So now that we have examined desire and emotions, let's look at the most important part of this strategy—the pause. The pause is the most important part of this strategy yet the most difficult. People want instant satisfaction and gratification, which translates into knee-jerk or impulsive reactions. To be able to sit with the feelings that you might have at the moment means feeling uncomfortable for a little while. Most people do not like discomfort. People also make decisions out of fear, or some need to control a situation often dreading the worst outcome. So they may feel a sense of urgency to try to control some unknown outcome by either rushing to fix it by saying or doing something without giving enough thought or allowing time to process. Yet to pause means to relinquish control at the moment to wait and see if the emotion will change. The emotions do most certainly change. In fact, sometimes they change as quickly as the next few minutes if you choose to shift the focus.

The pause is about self-control, allowing you to tap into your emotional intelligence to exercise self-discipline and the ability to exercise introspection and allow space to process. The pause allows you the opportunity to see the choices that you would have missed had you surrendered to your flesh and reacted. When you learn how to use "the pause button," you can now employ your *instead of*s. As mentioned before, you always have choices, and you should generate a list of them to use at your disposal; some may be general, and some may need to be specific to the situation at hand. Here are some examples of *instead of*s.

Instead of acting out in anger, I could walk away, take a few deep breaths, and slowly count until I feel calmer.

Instead of sending an angry email, I could save it in the draft and wait for a few hours to see if I still want to send it.

Instead of responding immediately to something someone said that hurt me, I could think about it differently and ask myself, Why would this person behave this way? *(This means learning to assume positive intent.)*

Instead of eating when I know I'm not hungry, I could drink a glass of water, take a walk, or call a friend I haven't spoken to in a while, so I can examine my emotion instead of trying to eat my emotions away.

Instead of calling an ex from an unhealthy relationship, I could write in my journal and process my thoughts or write a letter of self-reflection to identify concrete reasons why the relationship ended.

The *instead ofs* provide rational options and remind you that you have choices. *Instead ofs* teach your brain to exercise flexible thinking that there are many solutions to one problem. More importantly, the *instead ofs* remind you that you have control of the choices you make, which is a very powerful reminder in the process of managing your emotions. Here is a visual of what the strategy desire, emotion, pause, and action might look like.

Illustration 1.

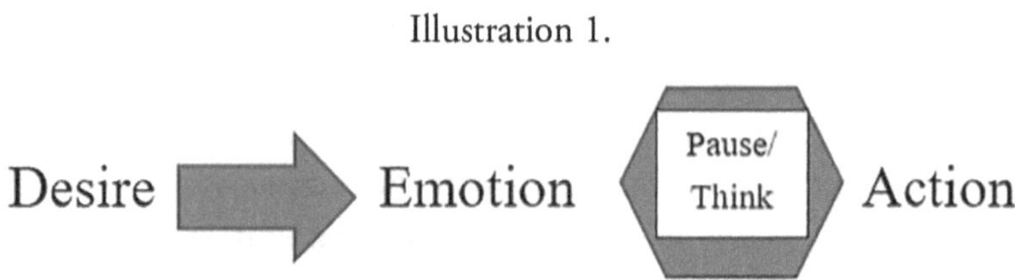

The Bible says, "do not be disheartened, do not be dismayed, for the Lord your God is with you wherever you go." Joshua 1:9 (NIV). That tells us that no matter what situation we may find ourselves in, knowing that you have the protection and provision of the Holy Spirit who is omnipresent, is an assurance of the attitude you should have and exercise in your life.

Considering the coal miners of Chile or any of the numerous stories of difficult tragedies around the globe, amid a challenging and uncertain situation, our perspective and disposition are paramount. If you are sinking in quicksand, the more you panic the faster the quicksand

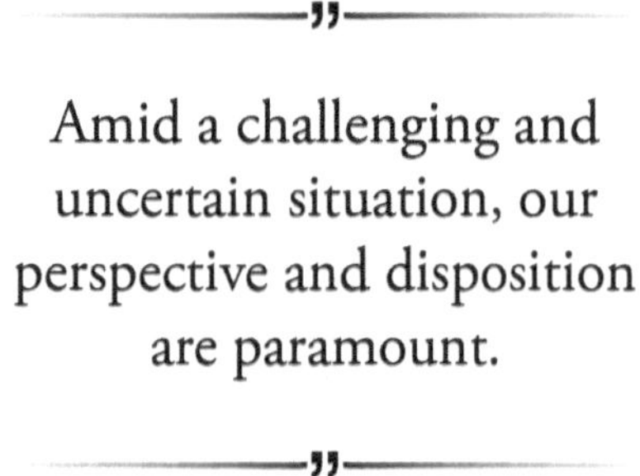

Amid a challenging and uncertain situation, our perspective and disposition are paramount.

will consume you. But if you remain calm and manage your emotions around what might feel like a justifiable panic, if the outcome will be what it is, wouldn't it make more sense to preserve your energy by choosing a better attitude that will allow you to think rationally?

If you truly want to be able to manage your emotions in uncertain times, remember these practical and simple tips.

1. *Learn how to become self-aware.* Self-awareness allows you to know when you don't quite feel like yourself. It is your internal barometer that lets you know your emotions are shifting or have shifted. This way, you can quickly self-assess, identify, or pinpoint what caused the shift and choose a different thought to help you choose a more positive and stable emotion. In other words, control your thoughts before they control you; manage your emotions, and they will not run away with you.

2. *Acknowledge what you feel.* Brushing away your emotions only causes you to sink deeper into them. Face them, acknowledge them, and figure out what choices you have. You always have options and choices. You just need to give yourself permission to feel what you feel but don't allow yourself to stay there, especially when your emotions are negative and will only lead to negative feelings and reactions.

3. *Recognize that all emotions are valid but must be expressed appropriately.* No one can tell you how to feel or how you should feel. You feel what you feel because you choose to feel that way. Therefore, because your feelings are your own, they are valid. However, validating your feelings does not mean you have permission to display them inappropriately. Recognize that you have the power to pause and process. Pausing and processing give you the power or control that you lose when you display negative emotions inappropriately. If you feel pressured to react or respond, simply say to the person, "Let me think about that for a moment, or

I need some time to process what you are saying." This is a truly powerful way of operating with grace under fire.

4. *Adjust your attitude and communicate.* You may need to check yourself at times because instead of verbally expressing what you feel in an appropriate way, you may just be doing your emotions, which is most often interpreted as "having an attitude." When you shut down or get snappy and irritable with others, they are reading your attitude, which may need to be adjusted. Most people don't speak attitude, and often you will receive more of the same in return. So adjust your attitude and allow yourself the ability and permission of self-expression. This doesn't always mean verbally. At times, you may have to withdraw to write down your thoughts, and you may need to express yourself through your art, like drawing, dancing, or even singing. Regardless of your preference, do adjust your attitude to improve your communication with others about what you feel and need from them.

5. *Seek informal and professional help.* This may be your first and last option in helping you to manage your emotions. There is nothing wrong with seeking support. Support looks different depending on who you are. Support may be a trusted friend who you can bounce off things. It can also be a community support group such as a church or spiritual organization. Finally, support could be formal where you see a professional such as a counselor or coach and allow yourself to be vulnerable so your own emotional healing can begin. The most powerful thing you can do for yourself is to give yourself the gift of offloading the clutter of the mind and allowing things to be clearer, allowing a pathway to options and decision-making. A professional can also help you to hone your emotional intelligence skills to improve your ability to manage your emotions.

Chapter 2 Application: Manage Your Emotions

1. Managing your emotions means being self-aware and having the ability to self-regulate while processing your emotions. What are some ideas you may have about how you can manage your own emotions in times of uncertainty? Jot down your brainstorming ideas. Think about how you can practice and apply the strategy of desire, emotions, pause/think, and action as described in chapter 2.

   ____

   ____

   ____

   ____

   ____

2. Reflect on a time when you let your emotions take control. What was that like? What were the outcomes of that situation or circumstance? What would you have done differently?

   ____

   ____

   ____

   ____

   ____

3. What practical tips can you take away from chapter 2 and apply to your current life situation? How will you do things differently going forward as you consider the choices you have related to the emotions you choose?

   ____

   ____

   ____

   ____

   ____

Consider taking an emotional intelligence test online. What do the results of your test tell you about the areas you may need to work on to manage your emotions much better? Take action by working with a counselor or a coach to help you make improvements in the areas of weakness or challenge.

Key Chapter Take-Aways

1. Learn the skill of self-awareness.
2. Acknowledge and communicate your emotions.
3. Adjust your attitude.
4. Learn the skill of self-regulation.
5. Know when to tap into informal supports and seek professional help when needed.

A Prayer for Emotional Management

Heavenly Father,

You have given me the gift of emotions. Yet in my life, I have misused my emotions and ignored those emotions I have that exist to help me live a more emotionally healthy and balanced life. Help me to make room for choosing healthier thoughts, which bring with them healthier emotions and result in taking healthy actions or exhibiting healthy behaviors. Help me to value the gifts of the fruits of the spirit: love, patience, kindness, self-control, joy, gentleness, goodness, and faithfulness. Forgive me for the times I have displayed negative emotions inappropriately and have impacted others around me in negative ways. Teach me how to be a better steward of my emotions. In Your name, I pray.
Amen!

Chapter 3

Manage Your Stress

*Consider it pure joy my brothers and sisters, whenever you face
trials of any kind, because you know the testing of your faith
produces perseverance. Let the perseverance finish its work, so
that you may be mature and complete, not lacking anything.*

—James 1:2–4 (NIV)

*If you are distressed by anything external, the pain is not
due to the thing itself but to your own estimate of it; and
this you have the power to revoke at any moment.*

—Marcus Aurelius

Stressful situations are all around us. Many of you live with stress on a day-to-day basis. Did you know that when you experience stress, it is based on how you perceive a situation and the reaction you then choose related to that situation? Two people can experience the same situation but have two completely different perceptions and reactions. One person may see the situation as insurmountable and unmanageable and find themselves in a state of stress so debilitating that it shuts down their entire human system. On the other hand, another person may perceive the same situation as simply difficult but could quickly employ viable solutions to help them cope and work through the situation. Same stressor, two different people, two different perceptions, and thus, two different reactions and possible outcomes.

Your body knows you are stressed even before you acknowledge you are stressed. The brain sends warning signals throughout the body to alert you of the very mechanism you have in place to protect you. This mechanism is called "fight or flight." Fight or flight means you either prepare to fight or prepare to flee.

As a child, I remember being afraid of dogs. This is because I was once chased by a tiny Chihuahua, which sent me racing around a car for more than a minute until I finally had the sense to hop up on the car to get away from the dog. I've been scared of dogs ever since. Whenever there is an impending threat, the first thing that happens is that the brain sends a signal throughout the body that might result in an adrenaline rush to prepare you for battle. The battle could look like standing up and fighting off a ferocious dog or running as fast as you can because you realize that dog is coming for you. Forget what they say about not running if a dog is chasing you. Luckily, your body can withstand this acute mode of protection and defense known as fight or flight.

We were made with stress hormones, but we were not made to remain in a state of stress and fear for prolonged periods. The body must go back to a state of calm after the crisis is over, and then the stress hormones calm down. But for many of you who are often anxious, upset, fearful, angry, very hypervigilant, and always waiting for the shoe to fall, this, unfortunately, contributes to trouble in your physical health. What is meant to be a way to protect you becomes more harmful to your health if the body remains in this state of stress. Simply put, after the fight or flight, your body resets to its *normal* state of calm or balance. However, remaining in a fight or flight state for prolonged periods does not give your body the opportunity to return to balance, also known as "allostasis" (McEwan 2000).

Behind the scenes, the body is working overtime to get you back to a place of balance to reduce those stress hormones. However, if signals aren't heeded, the body takes the next best route. This next best route might look like a shutdown. A shutdown could occur both mentally and physically. Mentally, it might mean because you are in fight or flight so often, without an exit strategy, you become mentally exhausted, lethargic, hopeless, and sad. If this is your state of choice for a prolonged period, it is also called depression. Physically, the body needs to also protect you, so it feeds on the energy reserves, but in doing so, it begins to affect your immune system, leading to more viruses such as the "common cold." You might also be more susceptible to hormonal issues, sleep disorders such as insomnia, heart disease, diabetes, high blood pressure, and unfortunately even stroke. Yes, stress can increase your risk for all these very preventable diseases and disorders.

Studies support the interconnectedness of the mind, body, and spirit. Stress affects the mind, body, and ultimately the spirit. Thus, the consequences you face because of stress depend on you. One very impactful story that you should take note of is what happened to my patient's mother who lost her youngest son to murder.

My patient, who we will call Emma, observed that her mother didn't seem to show any emotional signs of grief after she lost her son. The loss was devastating for the family, but her mother seemed to go on as if everything was fine. We should note here that people grieve in different ways. Some suppress the expression of grief or sadness, which can be quite dangerous to both your mental and physical health. Some people have a hard time accessing their emotions or knowing how to use them appropriately. Consequently, Emma shared that about a month after her brother died that her mother had a heart attack. This is a common phenomenon where a person loses a loved one, and not long after, they may become physically ill or even die. This idea that a person "died of a broken heart" is quite a real phenomenon. What was even more troubling is that several months later, her mother became critically ill and was hospitalized with a brain aneurism. What happened here? Stress! Not just stress but unmanaged and unprocessed emotions and stress symptoms, which she suppressed.

Stress can impact every part of our bodies. It is true that stress is based on how we chose to perceive a situation and the reactions we chose based on our perceptions, but there are some situations such as a loss that can be very difficult to process or even understand. With that, those who chose not to process that kind of stress, which could have a big impact on their lives, may find there are also physical consequences to emotional distress, such as critical illness as told in Emma's story.

Another patient, who we will call Adele, has liver disease. She was warned by her doctor that stress is not her friend and that she should keep stress under control and manage her surroundings and situations that can cause stress in her life. Adele's liver disease was in remission until she inherited the responsibility of being her sister's medical power of attorney after her sister was hospitalized during the global pandemic because of COVID-19 complications.

The stress of dealing with making medical decisions and the uncertainty that her sister could die took a toll on Adele and impacted her well-being. She felt that she could not manage stress having to deal with her sister's uncertain condition, her role as her sister's advocate, and the one who had to provide support to the family. Unfortunately, her sister passed away, which left her grief-stricken and also triggered the return of her symptoms from the liver disease. This again serves as an example of the mind, body, and spirit connection.

> To manage stress, you must pay attention to your body's warning signs.

Stories like this may cause you to take note of how crucial it is to manage stress. Yet we live with stress every day and tend to ignore the signs or fail to stay in tune with what our minds and bodies need until it is too late. It is necessary that you take practical steps to be intentional about stress management. As clearly illustrated in the stories about those who had physical reactions to unmanaged stress, it is so crucial *to know your body's warning signs.*

If we are present and mindful, we can experience the signals that our body gives. Warning signs can be headaches, chest pains, tension in our necks or other parts of the body, sweaty palms, tingling in our limbs, stomachache, tightness in our chest, and the list goes on.

These signals may begin as acute but, if left unchecked, can quickly become more intense and translate into something more critical such as an ulcer, heart attack, or even a brain aneurism. You can quickly counter the signals of stress in your body by stopping and breathing to decompress and doing so as often as possible.

Breathing is the fastest, safest, and quickest way to elicit the relaxation response to take your body back to a state of allostasis—the process that allows the body to regain balance. When you experience stressors on an ongoing basis and fail to achieve allostasis, the body moves into a depressed state or allostatic load, where it begins to seem normal to live in a "stressed" state. Unfortunately, without employing the proper resources to combat the dangerous levels of stress you may be carrying, you might feel like you are carrying a load of bricks weighing you down every day of your existence without any relief. This is not a natural state for the body to exist in. However, when you give yourself permission to take deep, intentional breaths from deep within the abdomen, you give yourself the gift of experiencing a flow from the body that feeds oxygen to every organ, fiber, and cell in the body, allowing your body to return to a normal state of balance.

Therefore, daily decompression, stress management, and relaxation activities are so important, especially if you can't readily change your situation. The good news is that it is possible to change the condition of your body and build your resiliency so you can exist and cope in an environment that may continue to be stressful. When you tap into your resiliency reserves found through techniques such as breathing, this allows you to be mentally well enough to manage your reaction to the stress.

When you are already overwhelmed and overloaded, adding more stressful situations to your plate is a recipe for disaster. *Learn to say no* as a tool to manage stress. *No* is a little word that carries with it so much power, yet for some, saying *no* unearths feelings of guilt. Often, your *nos* may not be solid, which leads you to spend so much time justifying your *no* that you talk yourself into saying *yes* when you really wanted to say *no*.

Depending on the size and impact of change, it is generally important to take inventory of the number of changes that are occurring in your life at the same time. Take caution not to make major decisions or other major changes in your life if you are already going through a big change. For example, if you are going through a divorce, it might not be the best time to accept a promotion and/or buy a new house. While those things might seem necessary, the impact on your mind and body that those stressors are causing might not be readily apparent. But the mind and the body are keeping score in the background and causing stress overload. While the adrenaline may be protecting you from feeling the impact, you are headed for a major train derailment, and you will eventually crash. The way you make decisions is also going to be impacted because of the compound stress you are experiencing.

Guilt leads to emotional distress that tends to be self-imposed. The longer you hold onto feelings of guilt, the harder it is to cope with life. Feelings of guilt also lead to stress reactions. Every decision you make when you are afraid or don't feel empowered to assert your *no* is based on guilt. This was the case with my patient who we will call Brandon.

Brandon lives with guilt which has turned into depression and despair. He isolates and lives in a constant state of feeling pressured. He states he cannot say *no* to the people he loves. He feels guilty because he feels that his mother never said *no* to him and his siblings while they were growing up. He recalls that his mother overextended herself to meet every child's needs even if she didn't have the means.

Brandon now feels a sense of obligation to his mother and his family. He believes that no matter what his family asks of him, he should do it even if it is to his own demise. How does one develop this way of thinking? This way of thinking is so deeply rooted that Brandon carries guilt or overextends himself to do things that he doesn't really have to do or sometimes wants to do. He turns all his emotions inward, and when he is not giving to his family, he is at home feeling sad or angry.

Depression has impacted both his personal and work life. He has lost interest in everything he once enjoyed. One of the ways used to help Brandon manage stress was to help him see the value in *regular exercise*. Exercise is another healthy and helpful way to release natural hormones called endorphins that help you combat stress and foster balance and feelings of calm throughout the body. It is like pumping much-needed air into a deflated tire to give you more miles to keep going physically and emotionally. Best of all, exercise has numerous health benefits.

According to the Centers for Disease Control (2022), adults should engage in moderate physical activity at least five out of seven days per week for at least thirty minutes daily. Exercise alleviates stress responses because it distracts you from dwelling on problems. *Avoiding dwelling on situations* that you don't have the power to change is a key tip to managing stress. Ask yourself: When has dwelling on a problem or situation changed that problem or situation? It almost seems futile and is, indeed, wasted energy to focus on things that will simply deplete your energy and produce nothing but more worries. If you have learned to dwell on circumstances and have difficulty getting off the worry train, it may be time to *seek professional help* to unlearn some of your catastrophic thinking patterns detrimental to your mental health.

As discussed earlier, stress can lead to problems in your physical health. Pay close attention to your body's warning signs and be sure to get the necessary health screenings and health care attention when there are changes in your overall health and wellness. Failure to take control of your health can and will lead to dire consequences, especially for health challenges such as heart disease, diabetes, stroke, or even brain aneurisms which are preventable illnesses.

What you eat can also help you manage your stress. Nutrition plays a big role in how well your brain functions, which results in how well you will manage stress reactions. When your brain is healthy, you are better able to process stressful situations, make better decisions, and manage impulsive or stressful reactions. Neuroscientists believe there is a gut in the brain (Harvard Medical School 2017). That simply means that what you eat will greatly impact the way your body functions.

A big part of your body's functioning is how well the brain sends signals throughout the body and how well the body responds to those signals. The nerves in our body connected to our brain are also found in the gut where food is processed. Eating healthy foods easily processed in the gut, sends the proper nutrients throughout the body to strengthen both the mind and the body to support healthy body functions. This helps you reap benefits in your overall health and well-being and will further allow for the proper management of stressors and stress symptoms.

Consider simple nutritional changes to combat stress. Some foods to avoid or limit are caffeine and alcohol, which significantly affects your mood. You should include foods that are high in vitamin D, omega-3, and vitamin E. These foods may include nuts, seeds, soybeans, and fatty fishes such as salmon, trout, and herring. You should also include more soy products, more plant-based products, and foods containing curcumin, known to help reduce inflammation in the body. Simple lifestyle changes may include replacing one or more foods with things you should include in your diet. This can give you almost immediate results.

However, intention and consistency are key. If you need help making nutritional changes, it might be helpful to consult a registered dietician or nutritionist. Overall, to truly combat stress requires a focus on total well-being. This might include a combination of nutrition; exercise; thought management; proper amount of sleep; focusing on mindfulness activities such as prayer, meditation, and breathing; open communication, and employing necessary resources to meet the demands of stress.

Chapter 3 Application: Manage Your Stress

Stress management might seem like a buzz phrase because we hear it all too often. But what is often easy to say is not always easy to do. We live in an overstressed society with what seems like daily compounded stress.

1. Identify your current stressors. List them.

____

____

____

____

____

2. On a scale from one to ten, ten being the highest, rate the degree or level of stress for each one of your listed stressors.

____

____

____

____

____

3. What can you take away from this chapter that might allow you to begin to think about your stressors differently?

____

____

____

____

____

4. How can you change your perception of the things that are caus-
    ing you stress?

    ____

    ____

    ____

    ____

    ____

5. How can you use the ideas learned in this chapter to apply to
    your situation now?

    ____

    ____

    ____

    ____

    ____

6. What is one thing you can change today that can help you see
    immediate results in lowering your stress?

    ____

    ____

    ____

    ____

    ____

7. What will you change about your eating habits to aid in better
    stress reactions?

    ____

    ____

    ____

    ____

    ____

8. How will you communicate differently to ensure that others understand your feelings and needs in a given situation or circumstance?

____

____

____

____

____

9. Is there a particular stressor that might require help or support from a professional to ensure that you do not keep ignoring the warning signs? What steps will you take toward action?

____

____

____

____

____

Key Chapter Take-Aways

1. Gain an understanding of the mind, body, and spirit connection.
2. Know your stress warning signs.
3. Employ healthy techniques such as regular exercise, deep breathing, eating healthy foods, and practicing mindfulness and relaxation techniques.
4. Learn to change your perspective—see the stressor through different lenses.
5. Learn to say no!
6. Don't be afraid to ask for help.

A Prayer for Stress Management

Heavenly Father,

Feelings of stress have overtaken my life and have left me feeling overwhelmed; overburdened; and, at times, depressed and anxious. I want to live a stress-free life, but it's hard living in a world with constant situations that are upsetting and overwhelming and, at times, incomprehensible. I'm calling out to You today as an act of surrender asking You to take control of all the things that burden me. I ask that You remind me to simply let go and allow You to take control.

When I allow myself to surrender, I can endure anything that comes in my life because with my faith in You, I can see my problems and burdens through Your eyes with the hope and confidence in You that no matter what I go through, I know that I can manage the way I perceive my circumstances and reduce the stress in my life because my trust is in You. I know that when I trust in You, there is restoration for me. So no matter how weary I get, no matter how stressed and overwhelmed I feel, You are a God who delivers, heals, restores, and will allow me to feel refreshed and renewed with every brand-new day. For this, I believe and pray in your wonderful name, amen.

Chapter 4

Develop an Attitude of Gratitude

Every good gift is from above, coming down from the Father of lights with whom there is no variation or shadow due to change.

—James 1:17

At times, our own light goes out and is rekindled by a spark from another person. Each of us has cause to think with deep gratitude of those who have lighted the flame within us.

—Albert Schweitzer

I'm reminded of a story I've heard many times, but it always seems to pierce my heart as if reading it for the first time. It is one of the most profound stories about gratitude.

A young man from a famous family was about to graduate from high school. It was the custom in that affluent neighborhood for the parents to give the graduate an automobile. "Bill" and his father had spent months looking at cars, and the week before graduation, they found the perfect car. On the eve of his graduation, his father handed him a gift-wrapped Bible.

Bill was so angry that he threw the Bible down and stormed out of the house. He and his father never saw each other again. It was the news of his father's death that brought Bill home again. As he sat one night going through his father's possessions that he was to inherit, he came across the Bible his father had given him. He brushed away the dust and opened it to find a cashier's check, dated the day of his graduation—in the exact amount of the car they had chosen together. (Van Buren, A., 1996 *Chicago Tribune*, 1996)

Gratitude is a very well-researched word as it relates to mental health and well-being. In fact, gratitude is a useful tool for coping in times of stress and difficult situations. Yet many people fail to use it because its purpose and benefits are often misconstrued. The thinking is that if everything in my life seems to be going wrong, why should I give thanks? Why should I be grateful? Why should I give praise? Gratitude is purposeful, and the very reason you may shy away from an attitude of gratefulness is the reason your mindset might not change when dealing with difficulty. When most people think of gratitude, they often think of having everything they need and want every time they need and want it. Yet that is quite the contrary. Gratitude gives you a way to focus on the things you might take for granted simply because your whole world seems to have fallen apart.

People who are grateful are more likely to experience peace in a situation than those who do not use gratitude as a tool. Even amid the worst situation you have ever found yourself in, shifting to a mindset of gratitude can temporarily shift your mood even at that moment. Gratitude, which comes from the Latin word *gratia*, means "grace" or "graciousness" (Harvard Health 2021). Grace allows a way out before you spiral down a rabbit hole of no return. Life will not always bring you sunshine and roses, but during those times when you feel like all is lost, choosing to think thoughts of gratefulness can help to improve your mood.

Even research on gratitude points to how people who practice gratitude on a regular basis tend to be happier and mentally and physically healthier than those who do not (Harvard Health 2021). Research also points to gratitude being a tool to help you recognize that some things are beyond your finite abilities. Gratitude encourages you to look beyond yourself to recognize there is a greater force outside yourself from which you derive grace or graciousness. This, in turn, gives you permission to give yourself grace every day.

My patient, who we will call Kerry, believed that everything she has or has ever had is a result of her own doing. She also believes that nothing ever comes easy for her and believes everyone else in her circle is always lucky to have good things happen to them, but her good fortunes come to her with a great deal of effort and hard work. Kerry suffers from severe anxiety and can quickly catastrophize a situation. This means that she tends to see situations worse than they really are. She has difficulty accepting that people will not always be to you what you might be to them. In other words, just because you have been a good and loyal friend to someone, doesn't mean they will be.

However, she is adamant about the expectation that people should return to her the same goodness she shows them and should recognize and validate her, just as she does for them. This mindset has kept Kerry in a constant state of despair, worry, anxiety, and feeling lonely. Kerry contends that gratitude is not easy for her. Because of this, Kerry cannot achieve consistency in her state of contentment or peace. As soon as one situation gets resolved or passes, Kerry finds that there is something else to worry and complain about. This has become the pattern of her existence.

To develop an attitude of gratitude, you must be intentional and consistent in recognizing the gift of gratitude and its benefits. If you have never considered gratitude as a tool, here are some useful tips and activities to begin your journey.

First, *choose to start a gratitude journal.* Starting a gratitude journal is as simple as beginning or ending every day by writing down three to five things you are grateful for.

Kerry complained about this activity as she felt that she would find herself repeating the same things. Even if this is the case for you, give yourself permission to start somewhere and build from there. Doing this activity daily brings about discipline and consistency, which reminds you to focus on the little things and magnify the positive things in your life, as opposed to awfulizing and catastrophizing things, which only leads to more negative thoughts and a dismal mood.

When you choose to put things in perspective, they act as anchors or simple reminders of where to place your focus, such as reminding yourself that you are breathing on your own, you can see the sun shining, you can hear the birds singing, you can hear your children laugh, or your limbs still work properly, and that you can feed yourself. These reminders are a great place to start. Even if you do have limitations, and have to rely on someone else for total support, what can you be grateful for despite your limitations?

> Develop and attitude of gratitude; be intentional and consistent in recognizing the gift of gratitude and its benefits.

During the pandemic lockdown, some people who thought about gratitude were grateful that they could still earn the same salary while working from the comfort of their homes. This was not the case for many essential workers or even those who worked jobs where their place of employment was closed. However, the next chapter addresses how many of the people who found themselves in dire situations of unemployment turned tragedy into triumph and are so grateful for the way they embraced change, which allowed them to find opportunities in dark situations.

Second, giving thanks is something that comes naturally for some people possibly because of how they were raised or socialized. When you *develop an attitude of giving thanks*, you recognize the power of praise and how much it is essential to say, "If not for the Grace of God." You are not of your own self, and anything can happen to you at any given time without you even realizing that you are next in line for something unfavorable or even favorable to come your way. Life brings with it unexpected twists and turns, and at times, these unexpected phenomena occur even to those who do everything right and good.

Certainly, no one deserves any misfortunes in life, but they come to us anyway. Matthew 5:45 (NIV) reminds us that "you may be children of your Father in heaven. He causes his sun to rise on the evil and the good and sends rain on the righteous and the unrighteous." This simply means that no matter who you are, things that you may not like or want can happen at any given time. Many of these things are outside of your control.

If not for grace, you could lose your speech, your sight, your limbs, or the gift of health. If not for grace, misfortune or harm would come to you, your loved ones, or even your children. "In everything give thanks" (1 Thessalonians 5:18 NIV). Recognize there is a force more powerful than you. Therefore, it is important to be thankful for all things. Giving thanks consistently reminds you of how fleeting life can be and leads to a better outlook on life's circumstances and situations. Giving thanks helps to foster a sense of hope and gratefulness.

> Gratitude is contagious; you become a mirror for others.

Gratitude is also contagious. When you carry with you an attitude of gratitude, others can see a peacefulness about you even amid a crisis. This kind of attitude is contagious as well as calming because you become a mirror for others. Gratitude also compels you to extend grace and kindness to others, especially those who are struggling or less fortunate.

Third, *choose to extend kindness to others.* Kindness is one of the gifts that comes full circle. When you chose to extend goodness to others even when things in your life may not be the best, that act of kindness improves your overall state of being. How is this possible you may ask? Allowing yourself to give to someone else the very thing you might need at that moment. For example, people who routinely volunteer in underserved communities or prepare meals for those who do not have them often report having a satisfying feeling of joy within.

Kindness can only multiply your blessing both physically and mentally. There is a biblical parable that speaks to acts of kindness. In 1 Kings 17:8–16, a widower and her son only had just enough for their last meal, but instead, she invited the prophet Elijah to her home and baked the last bread for him instead of feeding herself and her son. What happens next is where it gets important because Elijah blesses the widower for her act of kindness and tells her that she and her son will never go hungry because they will always have flour and oil to make bread. Her supply never ran dry, and every time she opened the jar, it was always filled with more than enough. Truly, the saying rings true that you should be kind to everyone you meet because you never know who you are entertaining or whose life you are changing with a single act of kindness.

Acts of kindness improve your overall mood, force you to focus less on self and your own circumstances. Engaging in acts of kindness, reduces your level of stress, simply by shifting your thoughts from your own circumstances to feeling a sense of fulfillment because you chose to help someone else. As a result, this sense of fulfillment can reverse any physical damage that stress and worry can be doing to your body.

During the pandemic, there were many who chose acts of kindness as a coping tool. Although we were all dealing with our own unique circumstances related to the pandemic, businesses forced to close, unemployment, uncertain economy, homelessness, separation within families, isolation, and the like, some chose to help others instead, finding creative ways to feed those with food insecurity or lend a hand to those who for safety reasons had to remain isolated. Giving gives you just what no one else can give to you—unspeakable joy. So make a conscious effort to (4) *choose your attitude instead of allowing your circumstance to dictate what your attitude should be.*

This is the hardest tip of all because most of our default is to allow the circumstances to dictate how we should think, feel, and behave. However, even in the hardest and direst situations, you can choose to adjust your attitude. Your attitude doesn't have the power to change a situation. Your attitude changes the way you think about your situation. Therein lies the power. In fact, choosing a negative attitude only makes the situation worse because of the stress a negative attitude brings. Remember, circumstance will and always does improve whether with time or a shift in thought.

Gratitude has many benefits and can be used to cope with mental health challenges. You should consider using gratitude as a tool to help you become more aware of things and others outside yourself, which leaves little time for sadness and self-pity. Gratitude stretches beyond just saying thanks and translates into our physical and emotional well-being. Studies indicate that when we are grateful, we are more likely to practice self-care which translates into better physical and mental health (Morin, 2015). Gratitude thwarts nasty, unkind, and vengeful behaviors. People who are grateful will spend less time thinking about how they can get back at someone else for hurting them but are more likely to rise above the difficulty or adversity, seeing beyond their own quest for revenge. Finally, gratitude and resiliency are linked. Gratitude helps to fill us up mentally so that we have enough in our tanks to bounce back quicker during times of adversity.

Grateful people are set apart because they understand the need to foster strong and supportive relationships. They practice self-care and mindful exercises such as meditation and yoga which can anchor you mentally and allow you to do quick self-check-ins on a regular basis. Quick self-check-ins may involve just asking yourself, "How am I feeling emotionally today?" "Why might I be feeling this way at this moment?" When used consistently, you are likely to maintain a mindset of choosing happiness or even maintaining a positive outlook on life.

Chapter 4 Application: Develop an Attitude of Gratitude

1. Start a gratitude journal right now by jotting down a few things you are grateful for.

    ____

    ____

    ____

    ____

    ____

2. Since you probably just wrote things down like, "my home," "my family," "my children," or "my job," I challenge you to stretch that thinking and write down why you are grateful for these things.

    ____

    ____

    ____

    ____

    ____

3. Now find someone that you are grateful to have in your life and write them a thank-you note. Be sure to include specifically why you are grateful to have them in your life and thank them for something they did or said that they may not even expect you to thank them for. Choose a different person every day or every week and write them a letter of gratitude.

    ____

    ____

    ____

    ____

    ____

4. Repeat this gratitude journaling every day and try to add one thing each day to your list that you didn't already write down. Introspection: After writing down the things for which you are grateful, take a few deep breaths and ask yourself, "How am I feeling at this moment?"

____

____

____

____

____

Key Chapter Take-Aways

1. Choose to start a gratitude journal.
2. Develop an attitude of giving thanks.
3. Choose to extend kindness to others.
4. Don't allow your circumstances to dictate your attitude.
5. Remember your mindset will not change your circumstances but will change the way you see your circumstances.

Chapter 5

Be Open to Opportunities

Lord, you alone are my portion and my cup/ you make my lot secure. The boundary lines have fallen for me in pleasant places; surely, I have delightful inheritance.

—Psalm 16:5–6

Opportunity is missed by most people because it is dressed in overalls and looks like work.

—Thomas Edison

You may have heard before that "with every disappointment, there is a blessing." Or perhaps you have heard it said this way, "Behind every cloud is a silver lining." Regardless of how you have heard these sayings, out of a dark unpleasant place can come many great opportunities. The pandemic forced people to choose more anxious and fearful thoughts. People were forced to withdraw or isolate themselves for safety reasons. Separation and isolation grew to become the norm. Yet for some, a shift in mindset led people to realize the under-

> Out of a dark unpleasant place can come many great opportunities.

lying opportunities that were brought about even during a time of great uncertainty.

People's need for connections seem to grow stronger as uncertainty about the lives of those around us seemed so fragile and fleeting. The threat of a loss can make people behave with more intention. Perhaps it was even the lockdown that made people examine time in order to recognize that they needed to carve out time to connect with loved ones and explore supports that were necessary to make isolation more digestible mentally and emotionally. As with human nature, the restrictions stirred a yearning for stronger connections. Even those who live lonely lives grew more aware of how isolation impacted their mental health and well-being.

> Opportunity met needs and morphed into the new normal.

If you stopped long and hard to think about your pandemic behaviors, you may realize how technology and a little bit of creativity helped you find more time for the people you love. God created us for relationships. Yet we somehow allowed life's demands to put us in a space of choosing possessions, positions, and status over people.

As numerous stories circulated in the media and the web, of how people gathered on virtual platforms for game nights, girls' night out, virtual parties, family meetings, worship services, and so much more, the new norm began to take hold. Events of these kinds taking place at record numbers even at a distance seemed to spark a new kind of thinking based on the human need for relationships, connections, and survival. Unprecedented forms of virtual gatherings quickly sparked a revolutionary way of socialization. Opportunity met the needs, and today, these events have morphed into a new normal.

Virtual gatherings, get-togethers, parties, and even church services seem to have entered the fabric of our social lives in this post pandemic world. People realize that they don't have to leave the solace of their homes to connect with others worldwide for the things they once used to do only in person. What is more, it has also become a cost-effective way to gather especially in times of hardship or when finances are low. Quite unheard of or even thought about prior to the pandemic was to have a virtual party or social gathering. Opportunity meets uncertainty!

Additionally, the global pandemic revolutionized the way people work and school. With the necessity for rapid change to keep the world of work and schooling from growing stagnant, opportunities for innovative technology and creative ideas sparked opportunities for the technological industries. Though global teams have been in existence for many years, work from anywhere (WFA) has taken on a new form. People are now able to work for an organization in one region but live in another area of the world of their choosing. Mass exodus from large urban cities to suburban areas increased the demand for spacious housing; this is the kind of freedom that has impacted the kind of work-life balance that people have been longing for but didn't quite understand how to achieve it. This form of flexibility and the ability to work from anywhere was rare or nonexistent for some companies prepandemic.

> Opportunity means that former resistance can lead to familiarity.

Fast forward to our post pandemic life, people who did not know what they did not know now realize that they do not want to be confined to an office or a fixed space to work. They want more freedom to work from anywhere as evidenced by work trends in our global workforce post pandemic (*Harvard Business Review* 2022). The most sought-after jobs are those that allow work from anywhere. Opportunity meets uncertainty!

Henry J. Kaiser said, "Problems are only opportunities in work clothes." Although you may be one who resisted the necessary changes that the pandemic presented, such as wearing a face covering in public, limiting in-person gatherings, getting your meals delivered at your door instead of delivered to your table, working and schooling from home, attending worship services online, not being able to visit a loved one in a hospital or nursing facility, seeing your doctor through a computer screen, delaying elected or nonemergency surgery, and even mandatory vaccinations, somehow you found a way to settle into and adjust to the way of the world—a new-world order.

Former resistance has turned into familiarity. Fast forward a few years, you may believe that the very things you may have resisted during the pandemic have become your right and entitlement. Life has taken us to technology overload, and unfortunately, this has caused some brick-and-mortar businesses to close or shift to online platforms, leaving some areas of the world looking desolate and destitute. People seemed to have hunkered down behind a computer screen where most of life takes place. One major technology industry has even revolutionized the next generation of the world wide web to meet the demands of the ever-increasing needs for the way we do life post pandemic.

The pandemic seemed to have thrust the world into a technological revolution, leaving those without the means or resources to be left in the dark ages. This technological revolution begs the question, was this revolution post-pandemic an intentional supernatural design thrusting mankind into his own social, emotional, political, and financial demise or was it more of an elevation to the next level widening the margin of the haves and the have-nots?

This calls for a mindset to (1) *reimagine your business or organization's infrastructure.* Reimagination requires willingness and flexibility and a step toward what is changing, or get left behind. This kind of change is necessary to survive in a post pandemic world and beyond. Waiting for things to go back to yesterday's norm is like living in today's reality with yesterday's mentality. Reimagination offers an opportunity to use the very thing you already have inside you to move into the light of your limitless potential if you simply take the blinders off and tap into the vast mind you have been gifted with from the creator.

Your limited focus tends to hold you back from your true potential. Stop focusing on the way things used to be, stop trying to reinvent the wheel, and focus on what is in front of you, the alarm bells of opportunity to be a pioneer in unchartered territory. There is so much awe and wonder that God has in store for us, and because we were made in His likeness and image, we have what it takes to be pioneers in this world. Sadly, we allow fear and the illusion of challenges and obstacles, which come in so many forms to hold us back from our God-given and God-inspired potential. Sadly, many of us die with unrealized potential.

People have suffered greatly from job loss, homelessness, sickness, death, and mental health issues, which seem to have ignited more worry and hopelessness. How can we ever get through this crisis? Yet there are many who despite experiencing the same difficulties seemed to rise beyond a place of despair and recognized their opportunities to create and thrive in a new normal. Some didn't have a lot of money because of job loss, but instead of asking, "What am I going to do?" they chose to ask, "What can I do?" These are two very different questions, the latter more powerful and actionable.

Some took what they had and gave it to the less fortunate in the form of free meals or meal delivery. The pandemic seems to have ignited more passion for giving, doing, and serving. This is because one of the most powerful ways to not allow your financial circumstances to get the best of you is to (2) *turn a passion project into purpose.* Even with little to no money, many have been able to take what they have and turn it into something whether it be a business, a side hustle, or a gift to others. Nothing can lead to something with the right amount of determination and a mindset to win.

Numerous post pandemic success stories exist. Some used their sewing and design skills to craft creative protective face coverings. Others recognized they could turn their passion and gifts into profits by baking or cooking now that the world demands more tasty foods and deserts, especially after brick-and-mortar restaurants that couldn't survive the pandemic closed. Some have found those very goods created in their own kitchen have now found a place in major grocery chains or department stores. Still, others saw the pandemic as an opportunity to think outside the box and propel their passions and gifts into entrepreneurial ventures. Some examples of these ventures included making scented candles which turned into a thriving small business or the booming cake and cupcake business which those who took the time to perfect their creative talent realized was a profitable industry for those who feed their emotions with a sweet tooth. Still, the business of food delivery propelled to standard worldwide behavior of having meals come to you right in the comfort and safety of home. What was the difference between those who emerged better and those who remained stagnant and defeated by the pandemic? The difference is in their thinking.

Though it may not always be simple to adopt a thinking of survival when suffering exists, a few key principles might be helpful. "All of us, like sheep, have strayed away. We have left God's paths to follow our own. Yet the LORD laid on him the sins of us all" (Isaiah 53:6). It isn't easy turning pain into triumph, but it certainly starts with a mindset of hopefulness and tapping into your resilience to hope for a brighter tomorrow.

So (3) *be willing to be open to opportunities that newness brings.* Think of newness as a chance to start fresh with innovative ideas and contributions to make life better for yourself and others. Ask yourself, What am I needing in a time of disappointment, sadness, or suffering? to see myself past my situation or circumstance…and what will things now look like for me? Am I simply looking for a handout, a hand-up, or a pathway to possibilities even if I only have a vision or a dream?

Keep in mind that although your right now might seem dim, with every brand-new day, there is a sense of newness, renewal, and opportunity. Wake up refreshed and remind yourself that it's a new day. "What opportunities exist for me?" If you are looking for an opportunity, you will find it. You must be willing, ready, and able to (4) *put on your survival thinking cap.* If you want to get past the suffering and live to tell the story, you must think about survival.

This is what British Naturalist Charles Darwin wrote about in his famous writing on the *Origins of the Species.* In his book, he believed that "organisms best adjusted to their environment are the most successful in surviving and reproducing" (Connor 2020). Using a survivalist mentality has worked in primitive times on up to civilization where we take what we have or what we know, and we use it for survival or to create a means of survival. When you take a step back from getting mired in the emotions of suffering, you realize how much you have that you didn't know you had. That things are not always as bad as they seem even when they *are* perceived as bad.

It is simply a matter of how you choose to look at your circumstances and what you choose to do about them.

Hope brings optimism and motivation. So (5) *be optimistic instead of pessimistic.* Looking at your circumstance as a glass half full instead of a glass half empty shows that you have far more resources than you think, and even with the smallest resource, you are bound to emerge with something greater if you simply put one foot in front of the other and keep going. When you open yourselves to opportunities, growth is bound to happen. Despite the pain from difficult situations, adversity creates opportunities for growth if you are willing to keep an open mind and grow through the pains.

An important principle to follow is to be willing to (6) *identify areas for improvement* in your life. A good example of this is what is often seen in relationships, where individuals may struggle to "own" their stuff because each involved is so focused on looking outside themselves at the fault and mistakes of the other person. In turn, each spends less time identifying areas where they can improve to contribute to making the relationship better. It is hard to look at ourselves because we believe that in doing so, it admits fault or flaws. The truth is, we are all flawed. When you can look at yourself introspectively and own your truth, opportunities you could not see unfolds.

After any shock to the human system, reorientation is necessary. What happens in an unprecedented event or one in which you were not prepared or didn't see coming would often seem to bring life to a halt. For some of you, the halt is longer than it should be because you spend a longer time in the shock of the event before things in your life can get moving again. If you lost a loved one, a job, or any other life-altering event, you can probably identify with the halt. But as you know, life continues. Life continues to happen all around you even if you are not prepared to move forward.

This was true for a teenage patient who lost her father suddenly, and even though he became sick with COVID-19 and had been hospitalized, from her perspective, he seemed to be improving. The family had hoped that he would be able to return home and had begun preparing his space for when he would return. Unfortunately, he passed away. I remember after some time had passed and this teenage patient returned to school, she became very angry as she watched her friends prepare for their senior year events and were all making plans for college. She could not bring herself to do the things other teenagers were doing and asked herself, *How can everyone just go on with life as if nothing happened?* The reality was that life had been interrupted for her but not for the other teenagers she existed alongside at school.

In some ways, she felt that everyone should feel and behave the way she was because what was happening inside of her seemed to be also happening outside of her. A key way to being open to opportunities is to do your best to (7) *resume or restructure routines.* Things may never go back to the way they were, and in fact, more times than not, they will not go back to the way they were. Otherwise, what would have changed? But in your new normal, allow yourself to resume routines to best adapt to the changes that have occurred in your life will help with coping and, eventually, thriving.

Not only has opportunities existed for us to pivot in our quest to adjust when life's circumstances force us to do so, but the most powerful opportunity that emerged from the pandemic, is the opportunity to focus on our mental health and to turn our attention inward. While teaching a class on antidepressants, one of my participants asked the question if I thought that the pandemic had anything to do with the number of people who were now taking antidepressants to treat anxiety and depression. As I reflected on the question, I thought of the opportunities that the pandemic brought about for us to shine the light on mental health, to face the stigma that has existed around mental health pre-pandemic, and how we have made unprecedented leaps towards narrowing the gaps that prevented access to care, even in environments where mental health care has been rare and at times nonexistent. The pandemic seemed to even the playing field around mental health, recognizing that none of us is exempt from facing mental health challenges.

We must acknowledge that many are unfortunately still struggling to collect the fragmented pieces of their minds to be able to cope in a new normal. The way we think about life will have changed forever, due to the trauma the world experienced during the global pandemic. When change exists on this magnitude as it did with the pandemic, it is important for us to recognize the opportunities that exist for us to pay closer attention to and nurture the mind, body, and spirit. We must recognize that we have control over our mind, body, and spirit, even when we don't understand the events of uncertain times.

Post-pandemic opportunities have created a consciousness of increased mindful thinking where we have seen how much emphasis is now being placed on mental health, and on creating spaces to talk about mental health in the workplace, places of worship, and in other public spaces, rather than just in traditional private spaces. Traditionally, people didn't feel empowered enough to say publicly, "I need mental health support, I have sought mental health treatment, or I am not ok." With so many people still dealing with the aftermath and impact of the pandemic, regardless of race, ethnicity, or socioeconomic status, it has lessened the likelihood of thinking of mental health issues as "those people's issue." Opportunities now exist for us to recognize that we all must prioritize mental health and emotional well-being. Post-pandemic, we have so many opportunities to raise awareness worldwide around the importance of prioritizing our mental health. The world's eyes are now open to how trauma can impact even the healthiest mind, if the proper mechanisms are not in place to manage stress, manage our thoughts, and maintain healthy supports and connections.

To be open to opportunities, you need to be willing to forge a victorious mindset—an "I can conquer anything that comes my way" attitude. To be truly victorious, you must take defeat out of the equation. Victory and defeat are not kin and cannot exist in the same space. How do you develop a victorious mindset? Here are a few ideas to help you be open to opportunities. Where your head is, there the rest of you will go. The hardest thing to do when you are going through a difficult situation is to think positive thoughts. The harder the situation, the less likely you will want to focus your thoughts on the good. The irony is that the very thing that can help you tap into your resilience is the hardest thing for most people to do.

You see, depending on the circumstance, to think positive means you are not being realistic about what you are really feeling. Some have even felt like they are lying to themselves, being fake, by choosing to be positive during a storm. But being open to the opportunities that tragedy and pain can bring means you will have to (8) *think triumph, not tragedy.* We can easily get stuck in our own self-pity, thinking catastrophic thoughts. The more the thoughts of catastrophe, the more it leads to catastrophic events all around you.

For example, you cannot think blue thoughts and expect the outcome will be bright, happy yellow thoughts. So if you want yellow, focus on yellow, and yellow is all you will see. Allowing time and space for feeling sad, angry, frustrated, or a mixture of those emotions is okay. It is healthy to acknowledge and process what you feel. But what is most productive and leads to better outcomes is where you allow your mind to go. So if you think you can't, you simply won't; but if you think you can, you always will. The more you think triumphant thoughts, the greater the likelihood that you will not be stuck in neutral or be on the road to a quick demise simply because of your mindset of defeat.

Some of you spend so much time still trying to figure out how to hold on to the yesterdays and why what happened yesterday occurred and how you can fix it that you miss the opportunities that are in front of you. How often have you found yourself looking in the rear-view mirror, wishing for the past that you don't even realize what is in front of you?

> Looking back, holds you back, but looking ahead, has endless possibilities.

You see, sometimes you must let go of what is done and what is gone to be able to fulfill your purpose ahead of you. Looking back holds you back. Even biblical teachings remind us of the dangers of looking back. In Luke 17:32, Lot's wife turned into a pillar of salt after being warned not to look back at the city of Sodom and Gomorrah which would be destroyed because of the evil that existed within that city. One might think that she looked back because of fear. This is often why most people stay stuck in the past, only to find that they do not progress or prosper. The new beginning can be uncertain and scary, but if you do not press on, how else can you reach the destiny that was meant for you? The road ahead may not always promise to be smooth and obstacle-free. But the road ahead has endless possibilities waiting for you to explore.

Chapter 5 Application: Be Open to Opportunities

1. Think back to a time when things in your life seemed hard and there seemed to be no hope or no way out of your situation. What opportunities existed that you now see that perhaps you couldn't see while going through the situation?

2. What did you learn about yourself based on going through the difficult situation?

3. What insights did you gain from chapter 5 that can help you now or in the future in challenging situations?

4. How can having an open mind about looking for opportunities within a tragedy be a valuable and useful tool for you?

5. What encouragement can you give to yourself to help you change your thinking about your circumstances or situation?

____

____

____

____

____

6. What encouragement can you give to someone else?

____

____

____

____

____

Key Chapter Take-Aways

1. Reimagine your business or organizational infrastructure.
2. Turn a passion project into purpose.
3. Be open to opportunities that newness brings.
4. Put on your survival thinking cap.
5. Be optimistic instead of pessimistic.
6. Identify areas for improvement.
7. Resume or restructure routines.
8. Think triumph, not tragedy.

A Prayer or Openness and Opportunities

Heavenly Father,

It has always been Your intention for Your children to live blessed and prosperous lives. We have gone astray and have missed the many promptings from You to live bold and confident lives, truly surrendering control to You when we ask for what we need and desire. Help me to have a mindset that aligns with Your will for my life that even in dry and troublesome seasons, I am aware that You are still good and have so much more in store for me. Help me to remember that when suffering comes, You have not and will never leave my side but that you want to refine and purify me so I am prepared for the tomorrow You want to give me. Help me to exemplify these practices in my life of keeping a faithful and open mind, delighting myself only in You and You who promises to never leave me nor forsake me, will grant me all the desires of my heart, and allow me to seize every good and perfect gift You have in store for me. In Your name, I pray.

Amen.

Chapter 6

Accept and Embrace Change

Come away by yourselves to a desolate place and rest awhile.

—Mark 6:31

Change favors the prepared mindset

—Louis Pasteur

At the start of the pandemic, my then ten-year-old son said to me, "Mommy, I think God is cleansing the earth." *Mind-blowing!* I thought, *yet profound*—out of the mouth of babes. Though this was, indeed, a statement that most would not be able to grasp amid such sadness, despair, and fear, some might even take offense to its implications. In fact, it is a statement that could bring about some anger and misunderstanding because of the many losses experienced during the pandemic. Yet after I had a chance to think about his statement, it began to make sense. It reminded me of the purpose of storms.

As scary as storms are to children (my youngest daughter is terrified of storms), their purpose is fascinating. Lightning from a thunderstorm is known to cleanse the air. No wonder if you are paying attention with all your senses, if you go outdoors immediately after a storm, often you can smell the cleanliness in the air. Similarly, change will always bring with it a degree of stress, but after the dust settles, it offers a sense of newness.

Stress is a natural reaction to change because as humans we thrive on habit. Change means having to get used to a new way of doing things, learning something new, or saying goodbye to something or someone we might not be willing or ready to. When habit or norm is disrupted, it requires a shift in thinking and behavior. Most people do not embrace the shift with open arms, even when the change is a beneficial and useful one.

> Stress is a natural reaction to change, but unmanaged stress has dire effects and consequences on our lives.

Stress can be considered eustress, commonly known as good stress like a birth of a child, a promotion, or buying a new home. Good stress is associated with good things although it might create a stress reaction like an adrenaline rush or euphoric feeling followed by a sense of fear. On the other hand, stress can be difficult, also known as distress, such as the loss of a job, divorce, financial problems, or a fight with a loved one. Whether the situation or circumstance producing the stress is something good or bad good, a fight or flight response will occur because that is our body's natural response to stress. When this happens, hormones are released in the body that can be harmful, especially if this occurrence is ongoing or prolonged without employing the proper mechanisms to combat the effects.

You see, our body is equipped to deal with acute occurrences of stress where we do things to bring the level of stress to a space of balance and calm. Consequently, if left unchecked or unmanaged and without the proper resources available to manage it, stress can have long-term effects on the mind, body, and spirit, in a form of hypertension, obesity, stroke, and mental conditions like depression and anxiety.

Stress can sometimes affect us in cycles. You may recognize there are stressors in your life but push away the thoughts or ignore the symptoms. For a while, this may work until another stressor surfaces. The new stressor doesn't counteract the previous one, but it interacts with it, causing you to feel more overwhelmed. This is called compound stress. You may think you are dealing with the stressors, but they are now mixed, creating an overwhelming force that causes you to feel overloaded and burdened, which may lead you to explode, sometimes during inappropriate and unexpected times. This might look like lashing out at your spouse, children, or friends. You may even find yourself during an explosion spewing things out about what you are experiencing internally, and the person witnessing the explosion might be clueless as to what you are saying or why you might have reacted the way you did.

Other times, you may implode, which simply means your body can no longer deal with the compounded stress and all the things you were holding inside that it protects you by shutting down. Shutting down shows up as symptoms of depression, such as withdrawal, loss of interest, and feeling hopeless or even helpless. People who implode and don't seek help may use negative coping mechanisms such as abusing substances, overeating or emotional eating, gambling, playing mindless electronic games to escape, overspending, trying to fix your emotions by using sex, inappropriate or toxic relationships to hide true or underlying emotions.

Unmanaged stress does have dire effects and consequences on our lives. Stress reactions are often a direct impact by how you are processing or not processing stress brought on change. Some may find themselves being very cynical or sarcastic because of the underlying anger associated with change. While others may simply stuff it all inside and develop an uncaring attitude.

A woman shared with me that after working from home during the pandemic and getting used to the freedom of being away from the office, she experienced a breakdown when she learned that her employer was asking the staff to return to the office. Her reaction was centered around, "Why are they doing this to us?" She could see no reason for changing what had now become her norm, and to her, things were working well. From her perspective, this was the world's new work normal, and there was no need to go back to an office that was probably physically unsafe.

Another woman felt that men were more likely to run back to the office than women. She contended that in her observations, men had transitioned back to normal with very few complaints, if any, socializing in the office and on break at coffee shops as if the pandemic never happened. She believed women had gained an edge in being able to take care of their responsibilities of parenting and managing a household while being able to work from home.

I began to think of the number of women who found it quite hard to do just that since it seemed to make the juggle even more stressful, not being able to separate their home life and work life, often hearing that everything seemed to bleed together in one day. There were positives and negatives on both sides of the coin. Clearly, the myriad of takes on the matter of change associated with return to work offered a mixture of emotions depending on people's status, gender, positions, and overall experiences with change.

Accepting and embracing the changes in our lives is necessary for coping with uncertainty. There are important steps you can take to accept and embrace change. Managing change means managing you. The person with the utmost priority in the equation is you. It is necessary to constantly self-check. Self-check in managing stress might look like asking yourself some important questions like, "How am I feeling? What am I feeling? Why am I feeling this way? What are my options for dealing with the emotions I feel?"

One thing we can all agree on is that no one leaves this world without experiencing change. It is a common bond we, as humans, will share whether we see it that way or not. So why do we often behave with feelings of shock, fear, and stress if the change is inevitable and ongoing? In fact, the moment we are born, we begin to experience changes until we die. Frankly, even after death, some form of change continues. But let's deal with the living who find it so hard to accept and embrace change. It seems that the more we fight against change, the harder it is to deal with. Are we simply hardwired to reject change or react in a way that produces stress? Or are we just operating from a place of resistance and fear? Are these reactions to stress a choice, self-imposed, or simply learned that we believe we should simply allow the emotions to happen to us instead of the other way around?

Fear will always increase our sensations associated with any process we go through in our lives. Fear makes it harder to cope because there is the element of the unknown. Yet no one has ever been able to control the unknown or to know what we do not know about tomorrow. We are not God! Some things are better left to the unknown as was intended. So doesn't it make more sense to focus on what we can control: our reactions and how we choose to think about stressful situations?

Humankind has created a great deal of self-imposed stress simply because of wanting to control what was not intended for us to control. Consequently, we foolishly fight for control of that which is outside of the

> Is your reaction to change active, passive, or stuck in neutral?

realm of our control, and we are left trying to figure out how to distinguish between the things we can control and the things we cannot.

When dealing with change, are you one who tends to be passive, active, or stuck in neutral? Perhaps for you, it depends on the nature and size of the change. Research shows that most of you will passively deal with change (Bridges 2019). You may not even choose to see the writing on the wall that change is coming. Do you run and hide, dig your head in the sand, or choose to deal with change only when it smacks you in the face and forces you into action?

Let's examine some key ways to help you control your reaction to change. We should all (1) *develop skills in planning and preparing for change* because although you may not experience the daily impact of the changes occurring inside you, they are happening nonetheless, and staying prepared is key. Louis Pasteur once said, "Change favors the prepared mindset." How can we develop a prepared mindset? (2) *Eliminate or overcome fear!*

A pregnant woman knows that at any point in time during the last few weeks of her pregnancy, her water can break, so she knows it is wise to stay prepared. Similarly, often those who spend time planning and preparing realize that it is smart to have a "bag" ready to go well ahead of time to avoid undue stress. This does not mean living with hypervigilance or fear; it simply means being wise, paying attention, and knowing when it is time to move with the changes or transition to the next.

People who run a business or have a business mindset know all too well that they must stay ahead of the change. If not, their business would not survive in this constantly changing world.

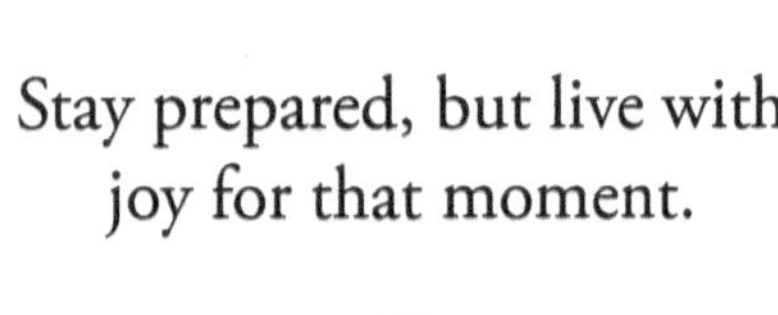

Market changes can also greatly impact business because of market unpredictability and volatility. Although constant changes can lead to a stressed mind, and there is no certainty in markets like stock, people still take stock in it and brace for the changes. You may have learned that if you take too much stock in volatile markets, you may stand to lose at times more than you've gained. Life is certainly a balancing act, and when it comes to changes, you must approach it from the perspective of staying prepared while living in joy for the moment in time that you have.

A friend shared with me that his uncle has a farm, and though he is good at farming, he has not kept up with the times. Thus, he finds himself struggling. He refuses to investigate ways to make his products available to a wider market despite his struggles. We have all heard of struggling farmers, but technology has been a helpful aid to those who have allowed themselves to learn and use the technological advancements available.

Let's take a closer examination of how we should think and behave in these uncertain times. People who save for retirement realize that they cannot wait until the year of their expected retirement to start preparing emotionally and financially. A ship never goes out to sea with passengers without having a lifeboat or life vests on board. Seamen don't go out to sea with the mentality that the boat will sink, but in each example, it is wise to prepare. Not doing so is simply foolish and irresponsible. Living this life without developing a mindset of constantly being ready to adapt to change is also foolish and irresponsible.

This life calls for us to (3) *develop a mindset of preparation*. This will lead to better coping and an outcome of resilience. When you live life in passivity, idle, with your head in the sand, change catches you off guard. You tend not to realize that things are constantly changing around you, and therefore, it is wise to live prepared and be ready to adjust and adapt.

Why do some people fear change? Fear is often fueled by a need to control the unknown or uncertainty. This is especially true for those who feel a need to control everything. In this case, often people with this need to have control over everything may lack the ability to decipher between the things they can control and those things they cannot. Change also requires work. When people get used to doing things a certain way, they typically do not want to put forth an effort to learn or get used to a new way of doing or thinking about things.

A good way to manage this need to control everything is to work on restructuring the way the brain processes things. Naturally, this is not an overnight process, but this can help you to better manage stress and how you deal with life. In every situation, you should ask yourself, Is this something I can control, or is this situation outside my control? If you are being honest with yourself and your answer, you will realize that 90 percent of the things you stress over are things you simply cannot control but still try to.

> 90% of the things you stress about are things you simply cannot control.

Another technique for those who get stuck in a vicious cycle of *what if*s is to examine two differing perspectives. The anxious mind tends to default to the negative. For example, when examining two possible outcomes when uncertainty is present, the anxious mind will more often align with the negative outcome or say, "This is not going to have a favorable outcome." But taking the time to examine the two possible outcomes might require you to look at the *what if*s from the perspective of what if it *does* work out.

One of my patients was stepping into new territory at work and all she could think about was failure. Instead of looking at the new challenge as an opportunity for growth and excitement, all she saw was failure. The project she was assigned took her out of her comfort zone and the resources she normally had at her disposal would no longer be present. The fact that she chose to think failure, forced her into rigid thinking where she couldn't even see the endless possibilities of how she could leverage the resources she already had to identify new ones in the new place where she was going to be working temporarily. The thoughts of failure kept her stuck and stressed. In the end, the assignment *did* work out and she realized she had wasted so much time and energy stressing over something that she had the power to chart the course in her thinking for a favorable outcome. How sad it is for most of you who spend your life operating in a wasted mental energy zone and miss out on the joys of the journey on the way to your next level of growth.

If you have two competing perspectives on the table, "What if it does work out?" and "What if it doesn't work out?" the more favorable option to focus your energy is obviously on the "What if it does work out." In doing so, you give yourself a better chance of keeping your cognitive energy at a higher level, allowing you to choose more positive emotions as opposed to those that are often draining and self-defeating when you choose negative emotions. What you focus on is more often aligned with the outcome you will get. So (4) *choose your focus carefully and wisely.*

The Baader-Meinhof phenomenon, commonly known as frequency bias or frequency illusion, might be an applicable concept to consider here. The phenomenon originally got its name in 1976 from a terrorist group known as the "Red Army Faction," and after this group successfully evaded German Police officers for years, they were suddenly popping up everywhere (Pietrangelo 2019). The term was later expanded to explain our "selective focus."

To understand this concept from a rudimentary perspective, consider your dream car or even one you really desire. Perhaps you have found yourself focusing your attention on thoughts of having this car, and when you finally got the car, you noticed that everyone else seems to have the car too. "How come I didn't see this car everywhere before, and now that I have it, everyone else seems to have it?" The answer is simple. What you choose as your focus will essentially remain in plain view or plain sight even in our thoughts and emotions. In other words, the thoughts you focus on will show up in your emotions and behaviors every time.

There is very little certainty in this life, except that we can be certain that we will be born, and one day, we will die. You will never know what you don't know no matter how much time you spend trying to figure out the things that lie beyond the realm of the unknown. Some things are purposely hidden to protect you or simply because you don't need to have that knowledge. This does not mean that we should hide in the sand or stay in the dark about knowledge. You should always have a thirst for knowledge and continue to grow as a lifelong learner. But you will never fully know some things. Most of us with curious thinking find ourselves in a cycle of "the more you know, the more you realize you don't know and want to know." However, uncertainty is one of those things that we don't have to try to control because it is not intended for us to control; we simply need to know how to cope with it.

Things do not stay the same. We can be certain that things will continue to change and evolve. Therefore, the sooner you embrace that truth, the more acceptance will come. Fighting against change depletes energy and valuable mental resources only to find that you will eventually have to join what has changed or get left behind. When uncertain things come in your life, which side of the change fence will you be on?

Chapter 6 Application: Embrace and Accept Change

1. Reflect on a recent change that has occurred in your life. How did you cope with the change?

____

____

____

____

____

2. What insights did you gain from this chapter that will help you cope and embrace change events in the future?

____

____

____

____

____

3. What kind of changes tend to be more challenging for you? Why?

____

____

____

____

____

4. How can you challenge yourself to embrace changes of any form or size more effectively in the future?

____

____

____

____

____

Key Chapter Take-Aways

1. Develop a mindset of preparation. Remember change favors the prepared mindset.
2. Develop skills in planning and preparing for change. Change is inevitable.
3. Eliminate or overcome fear. Fear keeps you stuck or immobilized.
4. Choose your focus carefully and wisely. Where your focus is, there goes your thoughts and emotions.

A Prayer for Managing Change

Heavenly Father,

Since the beginning of time, we have had to deal with change. If change is one of the oldest things that mankind has had to deal with, why is it so hard for me to embrace change? I know that I will not always have answers of certainty, but I can rest in You, knowing that the changes I am going through are always for my good. Help me not to fear change but embrace the wisdom of Your promises, knowing that whatever I go through, even if I find myself deep within the valley of the shadows of death, there is nothing too hard for You and that I can rest assured that You will be with me and comfort me in all things.

I am grateful for allowing me this opportunity to grow and evolve and become the person You have made me to be. I am thankful to You for giving me the freedom to choose and that when I am stuck, I can seek You first, for all wisdom comes from You. I accept and embrace change because it is all a part of Your perfect plan and will for my life. Give me the strength and courage I need to tap into Your wisdom as I go through this transition in my life. In Your name, I pray.

Amen.

Chapter 7

Lean into Your Faith

*Faith is being sure of what we hope for and
certain of what we do not see.*

—Hebrews 11:1

Faith is the gaze of a soul upon a saving God.

—A. W. Tozer

During the writing of this book, I lost my dear old dad. Talk about uncertainty. Death is certain, but the timing of death is always uncertain. Although my father's death was not sudden, nothing prepared me for the pain I felt when he transitioned. As a skilled clinician, I can walk patients through the process of grief. Yet when faced with your own battle with the uncertainty of death and losing a loved one, faith can be an amazing source of comfort. In fact, one of the things about death is that it can teach you a lot about embracing and dealing with uncertainty. No matter how upset you are as you walk through the stages of grief and loss (i.e., denial, anger, bargaining, depression, and acceptance), the one thing that you will never be able to control is the loss of someone through death, who is not coming back.

The images of my dad taking his last breath are forever etched in my mind. Sarah Louise Delany once said, "Life is short, it is up to you to make it sweet." I could still hear myself bellowing out that gut-wrenching cry as I watched my dad's body jerk as the breath and spirit left his body. His transition started early that Tuesday morning in January when I stood at my kitchen sink finishing up the breakfast dishes after my children left for school. I had a busy day ahead, but my mind was far in the distance as I looked out the kitchen window, watching the bright sunshine beaming in from my backyard. Little did I know that this was the day I would lose my daddy. I suddenly felt a presence come over me that gently and softly whispered in my spirit, "It's time."

As a natural reaction in my spirited voice, I sang out, "No." I finished the dishes and went upstairs to get ready to start my day and checked my phone. There it was—the text message that confirmed what I had heard from the Holy Spirit. The hospital had called my sister to ask her to get everyone together. They said it will only be a matter of time before my father passed away. We had to all get on the video call because that was the only way we would be able to say our goodbyes.

You see, many of you are probably all too familiar that because of the pandemic, the hospital was on lockdown. My father had to die alone without his family at his bedside holding his hands as he made the transition to the other side. Yet I am grateful for the technology that allowed us to be there, albeit not in person. The uncertainty of knowing he was going to die but not knowing when and trying so hard to accept the helpless feeling knowing there is nothing you can do is even more jarring. I still find myself at times having moments of wanting to call him or reaching out a hand, wishing I could feel his human touch, or even questioning the reality of never being able to see him on this side of the veil again.

What does it mean to lean into your faith? When there is nothing left to do, faith supersedes everything. Faith is like experiencing joy when you know in your heart you should feel pain. Faith is like walking in a hot and dry desert for miles knowing that up ahead is a stream of spring water but not knowing when you will reach the spring. Faith is also like navigating the darkness because you know there is light within you, and that light helps you to see even in dark unfamiliar territory. Faith is having hope when the world says, "Give up." Faith is like walking in peace when the world is at war. Finally, faith is living life with unspeakable and unexplainable joy because you know and understand what it means to have eternal life.

Most people of faith do not really understand what it means to exercise faith in times of stress, hardship, and uncertainty. Instead, most often, the emotions of choice are fear and frustration, anger, and even sadness and despair because faith doesn't always translate as easily

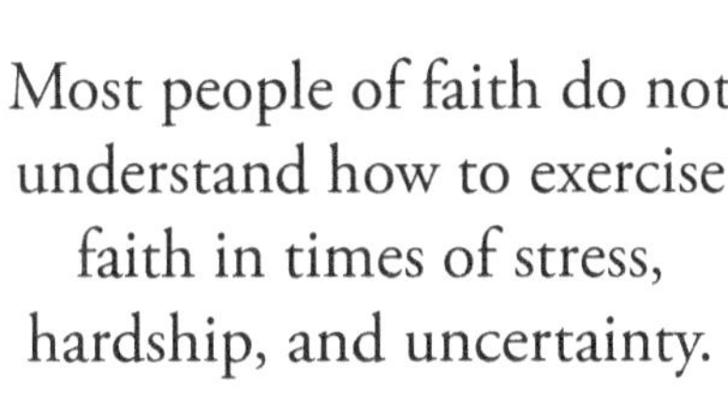

> Most people of faith do not understand how to exercise faith in times of stress, hardship, and uncertainty.

in the practical sense. It's easy to lose faith when lots of bad things have happened in your life or you've experienced many unanswered prayers. This is how it is with my patient Aubrey, who has chronic stress, anxiety, and depression. Aubrey said he used to be spiritual but has let go of his faith after getting divorced twice, struggling financially, and losing a loved one. The problem for Aubrey is losing his faith meant losing his anchor. He feels as if he has lost his grounding which left him without hope. So how does one exist after losing their anchor? They are left to drift into a hopeless abyss. Thus, opening themselves to living anxiously and uncertain. To say you have faith doesn't mean you will not be afraid. In fact, the psalmist writes in Psalm 56:3, "When I am afraid, I will put my trust in thee" (NIV). Clearly, God knew that in this life, trouble would bring about emotions of fear. Yet faith still stands. The courage to choose faith over fear is one that might be difficult for most even those who claim to have faith.

I remember having the very same conversation with a patient. During one of our sessions, she brought up a concern that she's afraid to let her child leave the home to go off to school. With all the mass school shootings and random acts of violence worldwide, you may echo her sentiments. Children are growing up today in a world where their innocence is stolen by the time they can say their *A-B-Cs*. She went on to say that at times, she wonders if she does need to insert a bulletproof padding in his clothing along with packing his backpack. She expressed that they say a prayer before he departs in the morning, and when he turns around to say, "Bye, Mommy," she fights back the tears and wants to yank him back inside because she wonders if that will be the last time she would see him.

I imagine that is a common reality for many. Yet I went on to challenge her thinking by asking her, "What do those prayers that you say with your son before leaving the house really mean?"

She paused almost struggling to find words at the thought of that challenge. In other words, when you pray a prayer of protection, are the words simply ritualistic, or do you really trust that the words that are lifted will serve as a covering and the rock on which you stand believing that those words mean what they say? I further challenged her by saying if you are going to pray a prayer of protection, do you not lean into the faith that those words will be heard and that whatever happens from there is outside of your control?

In other words, after you have said the prayer, your job is to believe and leave the rest. Believe that the prayers should serve as an anchor to keep you grounded in faith that what you believe in will come to pass and that your son will come home. I further challenged her by reminding her that even if she could keep him sheltered inside her home, she couldn't protect him from, or even herself for that matter, any other internal or external threats that may find their way to her doorstep. The reality that her fears originated from the need to control everything in her life and were the very thing that kept her anxious was keeping her from enjoying the moments of seeing her son off to school and celebrating the stage of development where he was. She finally responded by softly saying, "Good point."

Weeks later in another session, she proudly told me that she had been able to manage her anxious thoughts much better because that challenge has stayed with her. She further contended that she finds herself having shorter spurts of anxious thoughts and can quickly get her mindset back on stable ground simply because of being open to thought challenging. Faith helps us to challenge our thinking.

Nothing happens before it's time. When it is time, what will happen will happen. That may be hard to embrace, especially if you are one who has a need to control things around you even the things you cannot or should not try to control. So ask yourself this. Why do I need to control everything around me? One major part of struggling with things that are uncertain is the need for control. The more you embrace this need to control, the more you will remain in a cycle of stress and anxiety.

There is beauty in not knowing everything. Here is where faith comes in. Faith is like walking in the substance of hope and believing with all your might, despite the emotions, that you will get what you hope for, and if you don't get what you hope for, you are certain to get something better. The downside is not knowing when you will get what you believe and hope for. You may be hoping you will see your loved one again. It's comforting to be in that space. You may be hoping you will get another job or get over that breakup. You may be hoping that the world will get better, yet the world is as it should be. Even in those spaces, faith sets in.

Just imagine if you were given the blueprint to your life laid out exactly how things would unfold from start to finish. Many of you would jump at the chance of knowing what's next in every part of your life, how it will unfold, and how things would work out. Yet there is danger in knowing everything! What do you think would happen when you get to the parts in your life when there are things you do not like or want? Will you be willing to accept and embrace the pain, hurt, and disappointments knowing that suffering is a part of life? What about the difficult hurdles such as breakups, job loss, deaths of loved ones, family dissent, business failures, and even how and when you would take your last breath?

Most of you would try to manipulate and change the course of your life to fit the way you think it should be. That's not faith! In fact, that is what it means to be controlling. If you haven't already figured it out, being controlling yields nothing good and sometimes brings more trouble into your life than you need or ask for.

Needing to control everything in life is anxiety and fear. Emotions of anxiety and fear are heavy, leaving you overwhelmed and overburdened by things you cannot or should not shoulder. The beauty in not knowing everything means you can focus only on the things over which you have utmost control, beginning with you. Not having control of everything means you can surrender and take a break from always trying to orchestrate things in your life and in the lives of others. Finally, relinquishing control of things outside yourself means you can train your brain to focus on what you have in the right now, this moment, the present, and thus reduce anxiety, stress, and even fears.

Here are some practical nuggets to consider when leaning into your faith.

1. *Have hope.* You can choose how you think, feel, and react. Knowing that you have control of these aspects of your life is powerful. Ultimately knowing the difference between what you can control and what you cannot is the first step in embracing and using faith to cope with uncertainty. When faith is exercised, it allows you to *have hope.* When you manage your thoughts, you can choose the ones you want to manifest in your life and let go of the ones that will not produce good fruits. When you choose to have positive thoughts regardless of your circumstances, good feelings will always be birthed from those good thoughts. When you have good feelings, you show up in life more hopeful, more assured, and more confident. This kind of knowing says, "No matter what my circumstances are, I can rest assured there will be an outcome—good or bad." You can face every outcome with a clear and sound mind and find the best solutions based on how you choose to think. For every situation that exists in life, there are options. One of my father's favorite sayings was, "Whatever will be will be." There was not much he worried about, and even if he did worry, you would never know. He lived a very simplistic life with not much fanfare or not needing much.

> For every situation that exists in life, there are options.

His behaviors taught those around him to give themselves time to simply "be."

Faith empowers you to choose the best options and trust in your choices because your choices will be based on weighing all your options with a sound mind. That's what it means to lean into faith—to hope and trust that everything will be alright no matter how things might seem.

2. *Encourage yourself.* As you lean into faith as a source of support, remember that there will be struggles to keep the faith. These struggles may cause you to lose hope and abandon the commitment to keeping the faith. Give yourself grace as you anchor your mind and get back to a place of believing for the best and focusing on hope. This reminds me of the legendary story that has been told and retold for centuries of the "Tale of Two Wolves." In this story, an Indian grandfather set out to explain to his grandson how humans become challenged with a battle within them—a battle between good and evil. The Indian grandfather said to his grandson, "A battle rages inside me. It is dangerous, and it is between two wolves. One is evil. He is anger, envy, sorrow, regret, arrogance, self-pity, guilt, resentment, lies, superiority, and ego." He continued, "The other is good. He is joy, peace, love, hope, serenity, humility, kindness, empathy, generosity, truth, and faith. The same fight goes on inside of you and inside of everyone else as well." The grandson pondered his words and asked, "Which wolf will win?" The old grandfather simply replied, *"The one you feed."*

There is the practical side of the story and has been a constant theme throughout this book: What you focus on is what you become. Yet it goes a little deeper. Surviving the constant struggle within and arriving at a place where you love and accept yourself despite the struggle is where the other side of this inspirational story comes in. The Indian grandfather goes on to share with his grandson how feeding both wolves can yield a win for both. In the practical sense, it simply means paying attention to or acknowledging both the good and the evil that exists within us, thus forcing us to stay in a state of inner turmoil. But if we acknowledge even that which we do not like within ourselves and create a space for both to coexist, we strive for peace, and both wolves live. You see, the Bible talks about a time when both the lion and lamb will be able to exist together in the same fields without one devouring the other. Isaiah 11:6–9 (NIV) reads,

> The wolf will live with the lamb,
> the leopard will lie down with the goat,
> the calf and the lion and the yearling, together;
> and a little child will lead them.
> The cow will feed with the bear,
> their young will lie down together, and the
> lion will eat straw like the ox.
> The infant will play near the cobra's den,
> and the young child will put its hand into
> the viper's nest.
> They will neither harm nor destroy on all
> my holy mountain,
> for the earth will be filled with the knowl-
> edge of the LORD
> as the waters cover the sea.

God Himself knew that we would struggle with two opposing forces. This struggle between good and evil occurred when sin entered the world. Therefore, it is normal to have this struggle. But what you most focus on is what will always resonate in your life or at least become the dominant force. Knowing that the struggle exists is only half the battle. But choosing peace, in the end, quiets the battle.

3. *Encourage others.* The world and times are ever changing. With every breath, you are changing. You woke up this morning, and you have changed even if you cannot see

that change with your naked eye. But people seem to have grown weary of change. One might call it "change distress" or even "change apathy." The ongoing changes in this world have produced mass disturbances within the souls of people that they are acting out in unprecedented ways simply to communicate and protest the idea of a rapidly changing world that shows no sign of stopping or slowing down. It is in those moments that we need this tip the most: "Lean into your faith." You see, the world won't stop moving; in fact, it is predicted that more catastrophic and unprecedented events are yet to come, producing greater uncertainty that has never been seen before. But you can control how you navigate such events simply by managing yourself. The way to calm the storm within and to make sense of the incomprehensible is to lean into the only inner peace you can find, and that is through acknowledging and embracing faith.

The breath is the single most powerful human weapon. It's life-sustaining, and when it's not present, we are without life, suffocating and suffering. When the darkness of life consumes you, faith can help you decipher the illusion that is inside you which can keep you stuck and separated from the power of freedom you've already been given, the freedom of surrender that you can have when you breathe. Breathing when things don't make sense means plugging into the Source that keeps you afloat and will never let you sink. Keep your eyes fixed on the power of the creator who made you perfect and complete. Do not get stuck in the darkness of all that is inside you and holding you back from freely living and taking every step of faith that can lift you out of the darkness, created by the illusiveness of pain caused by life's sufferings.

We are all worthy of love no matter who we are, no matter what evil might befall us, and no matter what pain we've caused or has come to us. Though darkness and light are part of this universe, you get to choose.

4. *Remember the tide will turn.* God can bring good out of every tragedy. Always remember that He does not cause the tragedy because tragedy isn't lasting; it is only temporary. He does not promise that tragedy will not befall us here on earth. But what He does promise and does fulfill is Him being with us even in the fire, helping us navigate our way out of troubled waters. Rest assured, He never leaves your side, and that you can be certain of.

   Even uncertainty is temporary. This is because every tomorrow will come and will reveal itself to those who await it, bringing with it a brand-new day of opportunity, hope, and clarity. Because of His unspeakable love, He will always provide a way and a path forward if you keep your eyes fixed on Him. He will be the light of your path in this world of darkness. It's your choice to always choose the light that exists within you. Remember, "suffering is temporary, and it has an expiration date" (2 Corinthians 4:17 NIV). So (5) *let go, surrender, and just breathe!*

Chapter 7 Application: Lean into Your Faith

1. What does having faith mean to you?

2. In past experiences of difficulty, how has faith helped you cope?

3. Identify three to five ways you can use faith to cope with difficult or challenging times.

4. What insights have you gained from this chapter that can strengthen your understanding of leaning into faith as a method of coping with uncertain times?

5. Write down a prayer of faith or a mantra you can use to anchor yourself in times of trouble or challenge.

Key Chapter Take-Aways

1. Choose to have hope even when things seem hopeless.
2. Encourage yourself with inspiration and support from others.
3. Encourage others by lending a hand and exercising kindness.
4. Remember the tide will turn.
5. When you feel anxious or afraid, just pause and breathe.

A Prayer to Strengthen Your Faith

Heavenly Father,

I am in a mental space of trouble and distress. It seems that the fears have overtaken my ability to exercise my faith. Give me the ability to anchor myself in Your promises, knowing that when I pray and believe, I can let go of the unseen, knowing that You, O God, who sees and knows all things, will provide, protect, assure, and give me the grace I need for such a time as this. May I always find myself anchored in You. May I always hold on to the promises that You will never leave me nor forsake me. May I rest assured that even when I experience the things in life that seem unfair, upsetting, and uncertain, You are there, very present and fighting my battles. Finally, help me to remember that even when I walk through the fiery furnaces of life, and it seems like You are far away, help me know it is in those times we truly become one simply because You are carrying me through. In Your precious name, I pray, amen.

References

Beck, J. S. (2021). *Cognitive behavior therapy: Basics and beyond (3rd ed.).* The Guilford Press.

Bridges, W., and S Bridges. 2019. *Transitions: Making Sense of Life's Changes.* Hachette Books Group Inc.

ChipMonk. 2019. The Real Story of the Two Wolves. Retrieved March 1, 2022, from https://chipmonkbaking.com/blogs/news/the-real-story-of-the-two-wolves.

Cunningham, Conor. "Survival of the fittest." *Encyclopedia Britannica.* 11 Feb. 2020. https://www.britannica.com/science/survival-of-the-fittest. Accessed 27 March 2022.

Ellis, A. 2001. *Overcoming Destructive Beliefs, Feelings, and Behaviors: New Directions for Rational Emotive Behavior Therapy.* Prometheus Books.

Goleman, D. 1995. *Emotional Intelligence: Why It Can Matter More Than IQ.* New York: Bantam Books.

Harvard Health Publishing Harvard Health Medical School. 2021, August 14. "Giving Thanks Can Make You Happier." Health.Harvard.edu. Retrieved January 22, 2022. From https://www.health.harvard.edu/healthbeat/giving-thanks-can-make-you-happier.

Harvard Health Publishing Harvard Health Medical School. Winter, 2017. "The Gut and the Brain." Retrieved July 29, 2022, from https://hms.harvard.edu/news-events/publications-archive/brain/gut-brain.

Kaiser, H. 2022. Brainy Quote. Retrieved March 12, 2022. From https://www.brainyquote.com/quotes/henry_j_kaiser_101259.

Kershner, K. 2021. "What Is the Baader-Meinhof Phenomenon." Retrieved June 19, 2022. https://science.howstuffworks.com/life/inside-the-mind/human-brain/baader-meinhof-phenomenon.htm.

Kropp, B., and E. McRae. Harvard Business Review (2022). "11 Trends That Will Shape Work in 2022 and Beyond." Retrieved electronically on July 31, 2022. From https://hbr.org/2022/01/11-trends-that-will-shape-work-in-2022-and-beyond https://hbr.org/2022/01/11-trends-that-will-shape-work-in-2022-and-beyond.

Marcus Aurelius, E.O.R. *The Thoughts of Marcus Aurelius Antoninus*. Edited by D. Estes. 1908. [Boston, D. Estes] [Pdf]. Retrieved from the Library of Congress, https://www.loc.gov/item/08021626/.

McEwan, B. 2000. "Allostasis and Allostatic Load: Implications for Neuropsychopharmacology." Retrieved July 28, 2022. From https://www.nature.com/articles/1395453.

Morin, A. 2015. "7 Scientific Proven Benefits of Gratitude." *Psychology Today*. Retrieved January 27, 2022. From https://www.psychologytoday.com/us/blog/what-mentally-strong-people-dont-do/201504/7-scientifically-proven-benefits-gratitude.

Pietrangelo, A. 2019. "What the Meinhof Phenomenon Is and Why You May See It Again…and Again." Retrieved electronically July 21, 2022. From https://www.healthline.com/health/baader-meinhof-phenomenon#why-that-name.

Tobar, H. 2014. *Deep Down Dark: The Untold Story of 33 Men Buried in a Chilean Mine, and the Miracle That Set Them Free*. Harper Perennial.

About the Author

With over twenty-five years of experience as a clinician, consultant, life coach, and national and international speaker, Dr. Dacia P. Hastings Proctor, also known as TheTalkDr., is the author of this amazing book and resource. Her experiences are in the areas of public speaking, leadership and management, wellness coaching, consulting, counseling, and psychotherapy.

She is the President and CEO of DPH Consulting Services, PC, and is a licensed psychotherapist in private practice in the Washington, DC metro area where she helps hundreds of people sort out personal and professional life matters. She also consults with organizations on effectiveness with programs, planning, and employee development. She is the creator of StressFreeTalkRx, a digital download offering mindfulness support, and of a video podcast on YouTube—PowerTalks with TheTalkDr featuring AskTheTalkDr Live.

Dr. Hastings Proctor's professional experiences have been in the areas of organizational consultation, research, ethics, higher education, leadership and management, professional development, staff development training, team building, organizational effectiveness, executive and life coaching, curriculum development, motivational and keynote speaking, program evaluation, psychotherapy, employee assistance program (EAP), work life and wellness, child welfare, clinical assessments and interpretation, mental health and wellness, substance abuse, EAP counseling, HIV/AIDS, and social work.

On a personal level, Dr. Hastings Proctor is a wife and mother of 3 children. In her spare time, she enjoys spending quality time with her family, cooking healthy meals, running, yoga, mindfulness meditation, and traveling.

To contact the author, Dr. Dacia P. Hastings Proctor, or for more information and assistance, visit www.thetalkdr.com or email her at dacia.hastings@gmail.com